D o u B l e

D0247815

DELALICIOUS

A FULL PLATE
FOR A FULL LIFE

Sinéad Delahunty's farming background in Fethard, County Tipperary, inspired her passion for fresh ingredients. A Chartered Physiotherapist with the HSE in Dublin, she also plays Gaelic football with her Dublin club, Foxrock-Cabinteely and has represented Tipperary for many years at inter-county level. After the football field and the hospital, the kitchen is where you will find her, creating exciting dishes for her food blog *Delalicious*, which represented Ireland at the 2015 Cono Sur Food Bloggers Final in Paris and was named a Top 5 Irish Food Blog at the Irish Blog Awards 2016. She spent 2017 on a career break, backpacking across the globe, experiencing different cultures and cuisines.

Stay up to date with Sinéad at:

 www.delalicious.com    @delaliciousfood

 @delaliciousfood   @delaliciousfood

DELALICIOUS

A FULL PLATE
FOR A FULL LIFE

Sinéad Delahunty

The Collins Press

To all the Delas in my life: Mam, Dad, Eoin and Brian
– my family and constant supporters, thanks for everything!

FIRST PUBLISHED IN 2018 BY
The Collins Press
West Link Park
Doughcloyne
Wilton
Cork
T12 N5EF
Ireland

© Sinéad Delahunty 2018

Sinéad Delahunty has asserted her moral right to be identified as the author of this work
in accordance with the Irish Copyright and Related Rights Act 2000.

All rights reserved.
The material in this publication is protected by copyright law. Except as may be permitted by
law, no part of the material may be reproduced (including by storage in a retrieval system) or
transmitted in any form or by any means, adapted, rented or lent without the written permission
of the copyright owners. Applications for permissions should be addressed to the publisher.

A CIP record for this book is available from the British Library.

Paperback ISBN: 978-1-84889-338-2

Design and typesetting by Bright Idea
Typeset in Roboto Slab
Printed in Poland by Białostockie Zakłady Graficzne SA

Cover photographs
Front: Sinéad at work in the kitchen (Jennifer Opperman)
Back, from top: Beetroot, feta and black bean burger (Aidan Crawley);
cupcake quiches (Aidan Crawley); dark chocolate beetroot cake (Jennifer Oppermann)

Contents

Introduction   1

    Tips and Tricks   13

    Your Health Is Your Wealth   21

    Kitchen Essentials   24

    Using My Book   26

Recipes

    Breakfast   29

    Baking   55

    Tasty Extras   79

    Soups   91

    Super Salads   109

    The Main Affair   135

    Snacks   177

    Delalicious Desserts   187

References   206

Acknowledgements   207

Converting Ingredient Quantities   208

Thank You   209

Index   211

INTRODUCTION

DELALICIOUS is my food blog and how I like to share my kitchen creations with the world. Blogging was an unknown world to me until I finally plucked up the courage in February 2015. After a few quick button clicks, *Delalicious* was suddenly launched and I haven't looked back since. To say it's been a whirlwind would be an understatement!

I'm a full-time physiotherapist, Gaelic footballer, daughter, sister, friend and lover of food. So you might wonder how I can find the time to cook. The answer isn't a simple one but I have attempted to share my tips and solutions through these pages. I believe that if I can find the time to cook, then so can you.

THE BEGINNING

My family tree traces a long line of farmers and home cooks from rural Tipperary. I live in the heart of the Golden Vale, an area renowned for its fertile land and food in Ireland so it's really no surprise that both are embedded in my life. On our farm we raise beef cattle and grow seasonal crops while my dad also runs a livestock haulage business.

As a farmer's daughter, helping out on the farm is an inevitable part of life for me. From a very young age, my two brothers and I helped out doing farm chores but more often than not we were off exploring the neighbouring woods and forests. Climbing onto hay bales, riding in the combine harvester, raiding the hedgerows for blackberries, painting gates, picking stones and helping with the silage was how my childhood summers were spent.

Growing up in the countryside, most families have pets but my mam has an innate fear of all cats and dogs so that option was out. However, just as I started secondary school, we decided to get laying hens and they've been the most successful pets to date. Our hens can be temperamental but they do provide us with the freshest and tastiest eggs I've ever eaten. They also double as being our own personal food-waste controllers.

Not only did I help out on the farm from a very young age but also in the kitchen. My mam tells a story of me, aged three, balancing on a stool so that I could reach the worktop, wearing a little apron and chopping carrots.

Like many kids growing up, I initially fell in love with baking. I frequently ended up with half the cake on my face and clothes before it was even baked because who hasn't licked the bowl clean? A niche market amongst my classmates caught my eye and I sold chocolate chip cookies for about a week in third class. However, my chocolate chip cookie empire stalled after I discovered quickly that the profit margins didn't add up!

My mam's passion for food and use of simple, seasonal ingredients has always been with me. I was fortunate to return home from school every evening to a hot dinner on the table. Pre-packaged shop-bought dinners or ready-to-go ingredients from a tin or jar simply didn't exist in our house – so it was completely natural for me to continue making everything from scratch. It wasn't until I moved out of home to study physiotherapy in Dublin that, for the first time, I had to really fend for myself in the kitchen.

During my college years, I continued my school habit of bringing a packed lunch with me daily. Many one-pot wonders were created to varying degrees of success, using whatever lurked in the corners of the fridge and cupboards. College summers spent in India and America continued my culinary adventures, opening my eyes to many different flavours and ingredients, but also to the dietary extremes of the world.

After I graduated, full-time employment for a physiotherapist was scarce so I spent over a year juggling multiple roles, including three jobs a week on top of playing club and county football. This is where I learned the importance of a healthy diet. Long periods were spent travelling in the car and the allure of petrol-station snacks when boredom set in was all too enticing. Thankfully, in 2014 I gained full-time employment as a physiotherapist in a Dublin hospital. I finally had one job and one sport to focus on.

A SPORTING LIFE

Growing up in the countryside was brilliant and a strong, active lifestyle was ingrained in my daily life from a very young age. Every evening after school was spent outside kicking a ball, searching for lost sliotars or tennis balls, climbing trees, helping in the garden and being ferried to and from swimming, dancing, horse riding and athletics … name a sport and my brothers and I probably played it! With an established base of flexibility, hand–eye coordination and stamina, I had a good start when I decided to pursue Gaelic football towards the end of primary school.

GAA sports, and in particular football, weren't something at which I was instantly gifted. I didn't play or train with a team until I was eight or nine and many years were spent in goal for my brothers, because they didn't think I could strike a ball. My home parish, Fethard, is predominantly a football club so naturally this was the main sport available. However, a girls' underage team and ladies' Gaelic football club were only in development, so I started playing initially on the boys' team. Playing amongst the boys wasn't anything new to me after years of standing in goal for my brothers at home but now I could finally play outfield. It took (and still takes) hours of soloing, kicking, blocking and hand-passing at home and in training to fine-tune my talents.

I clearly remember my excitement when a call came inviting me to attend trials for the Tipperary under-16 team. We were driving home from visiting relations and I think Mam nearly crashed the car due to me screaming with joy once I put the phone down. All those hours practising my skills paid off: I attended the trials and the rest is history. I got the opportunity to represent Tipperary at both underage and adult level. I have been fortunate to play with some of the country's most talented players over the years with Presentation Secondary School, Ballingarry, University College Dublin, various Tipperary county teams and my clubs: Fethard, Tir na nÓg, Boston and Foxrock-Cabinteely (with whom I'm celebrating our first Leinster Senior club championship win in 2015, below).

LIFE LESSONS

Sport has taught me many lessons in life. I have learned a lot about myself as a person, including:

- how to deal with the heartache of defeat,
- the exhilaration of success,
- the skills to motivate both myself and others,
- how to lead a group of contemporaries by example,
- to have self-confidence,
- how to pick up the pieces on the field when all around you are falling apart,
- and, most importantly, how to believe in myself.

If you don't believe in yourself, who will?

Belief, to me, is the key to success – as the saying goes, 'You have got to believe to achieve', and this really is true. Dreams can become reality when you write them down, set a plan and follow through each step until that dream is realised. Not every dream or plan will be achieved on time or will be successful so don't be hard on yourself. Ultimately, dreams are all about the journey; you will know that you have worked hard and achieved, no matter how big or small the result. You will have grown and developed yourself along the way.

Experiencing the buzz of a victory is something special. Days like the Intermediate All-Ireland final in 2008 with Tipperary (opposite) and winning back-to-back Dublin Senior County and Leinster Championships with Foxrock-Cabinteely will live long in my memory. The friendships and bonds I have developed over the years through sport are ultimately the true reward for all the tough training sessions, heartache in defeat and commitment to the cause.

It is hard to put into words what football and sport mean to me. They are such a big part of my life and have always been a cornerstone when times got a bit tough; there was always a ball to be kicked and a team to be a part of. Even when the season ends, there's a period that I cherish for a few weeks and then I feel like I've had enough and it's back to training and spending time with all my friends and teammates.

Ultimately, I think sport and an active lifestyle should be fostered in every childhood. The skills you learn are life-enhancing and transferable to every walk of life.

THE BLOG

When I secured my full-time physiotherapy job in Dublin I suddenly discovered I had a lot of spare time. I like to keep busy so naturally I had to find something else to do and along came cooking and blogging! To call myself a food blogger was never my intention. The blog was created in an attempt to stop my older brother Eoin from annoying me. He had observed, tasted and criticised many of my kitchen creations. Not only was it an effort to feed myself, my family and my friends but, as Eoin thought, to share these creations with the world.

Initially I was petrified. Who would read it, was my big question. Followed by, why would they read my blog? His not-so-subtle hints about starting a blog eventually wore me down and *Delalicious* was born for the world to see.

My inspiration for cooking comes from everywhere – eating out, observing lunch trends of colleagues, cookery programmes, cookbooks, social media and magazines. I adore magazines and particularly the weekend supplement food sections. I devour them, ripping out sections and stashing them in folders for later inspiration.

Cooking, for me, is a passion and one that I love to indulge in and use to express my creativity. I am very much a visual and hands-on learner in life and this doesn't change in the kitchen. Trying and learning new things excites me and I will always jump at every opportunity. I love to taste and explore new food whilst travelling the world, learn skills at workshops showcasing different cooking techniques or cuisines and visit local producers, constantly soaking up knowledge and inspiration.

Not everything I have attempted or created in the kitchen has turned out as planned but that's where patience, perseverance and practice come into play. Sport has taught me that you must learn from your mistakes, and cooking is no different.

Pick yourself up, dust off the flour,
clean the pots and start again!

Blogging has opened numerous doors that I am very grateful and proud to have experienced. Representing Ireland at the Cono Sur Food Bloggers final in Paris, being named a Top 5 Irish Food Blog at the Irish Blog Awards and finally this book have been personal highlights. From day one of the blog, people would joke, saying, 'You'll have a book next' or 'When's the book out?' but never in my wildest dreams did I think it would actually happen. The process of writing these pages, creating and shooting the recipes has taught me loads about myself as a person. I have learned the importance of collaboration and asking for help.

ASKING FOR HELP

As a physiotherapist and sportsperson, the importance of a team and being a cog in a well-oiled machine is a natural part of my daily life. Blogging is very much an individual pursuit where there is no safety net, no captain to look to for motivation or manager on the sideline ready to call you ashore when it's not your day.

Asking for help is central to success. It can feel like a big deal to the asker but absolutely nothing to the helper. The worst that can happen is the person you ask will say no, but my experience has shown me that people are willing and delighted to offer assistance, guidance and a helping hand, however big or small. No matter what it is in life, sometimes all you need to do is let your thoughts out, discuss those fears and feelings with someone, ask for help and put a plan in place for the future.

MY FOOD PHILOSOPHY

As I spend all day in a uniform of sorts, be it working in the hospital or on the football field, fashion isn't my strong point and I am certainly not a slave to trends. The same can be said for my food. My recipes don't follow any strict diet as I have never followed one. I simply fill my plate or lunchbox with a healthy balance of food. Yes, my recipes are a bit more adventurous than the meat, two veg and spuds I grew up on but both types of meal are made from scratch with wholesome, unprocessed and seasonal ingredients. That's the only food I know, and all I think anyone should know.

As a sportswoman, I learned how nutrition and hydration are key components to complement athletic ability. Carbohydrate loading is necessary but when the common example of a plateful of pasta and chicken mid-morning before a game isn't your meal of choice, your imagination comes into action.

As a physiotherapist, I have witnessed how the way we move and nourish our bodies can have a direct impact on our health. Maintaining a balance between movement and nourishment can be difficult but not unrealistic to achieve. Small, consistent changes over time can have a positive impact on disease, illness and overall well-being.

Keeping a healthy balance is not easy with the availability of heavily processed food and the many ways in which physical activity is not required in our daily lives. I love to try out new ingredients that come to Irish shores and especially grains like quinoa and bulgur wheat that are used daily in other cultures. Many people think I am a vegetarian but I most certainly am not: I just love vegetables, so you will see them cropping up in lots of recipes – even in a dessert!

Moderation of sugar can be difficult both to achieve and maintain. Like most people, I love a sweet treat, but I try to replace sugar with alternatives or eliminate it where I can. Some recipes, for me, shouldn't be tampered with, like my White Chocolate and Raspberry Cheesecake (see page 188) and Meringue Kisses (see page 200), but these are special-occasion treats.

However, I don't give out to myself when I have a couple of chocolates instead of one. This is counter-productive and only leaves me feeling down. I opt for elimination at home: when I go grocery shopping, sweets and chocolates are not on my list. I find having at least one option from my desserts or baked treats on hand in the freezer for when I feel the urge for something sweet is a great idea. Likewise, eating out is a real pleasure for me and I will definitely have a dessert if one catches my eye on the menu.

I make, and encourage others to make, a concerted effort daily to choose healthy food and move our bodies as nature intended. That's why I like to use the Athlete Plate to check that I'm creating a balanced plate of food depending on my activity level that day. The Athlete Plate is a very useful visual aid that I discuss in depth later (see page 16).

My wish is that you use this book to nourish yourself and others, to treat your favourite people to some delights and to fuel your life even when you already have a really full plate.

TIPS AND TRICKS
MEAL PLANNING AND PREPARATION

Social media allows people to share how they plan and prepare their meals. This is a long-established practice and nothing new but it is a great way to ensure you eat what you want every day.

One of the big things that people often think about meal planning and preparation is that you eat the same thing every day. I certainly don't and then I get asked, 'Do you go home and cook every evening?' The answer is no. When I am in the kitchen, I generally cook a few things together, such as a soup, a curry and a hummus. Then I will freeze portions of them all, keeping one or two portions fresh in the fridge for the week ahead. Therefore, I have a stock on hand for the days when I am really short on time to prepare food.

Doing a weekly shop at the beginning of the week is a great way to focus you, depending on your week ahead and social plans. Always shop with a list; this will keep you concentrated on exactly what you need. Salad items and fruit are always top of my list; both will generally last two weeks in the fridge and will ensure you have breakfast, lunch and dinner well covered by simply adding some protein or a carbohydrate source. Plan ahead and chop vegetables, keeping some portions in the fridge whilst freezing others to ensure a constant supply.

Likewise, I generally buy meat and fish once a month in big batches and freeze from fresh. Taking as little as half an hour each evening to prepare your breakfast and lunch for the day ahead is well worth it, for both your pocket and health.

FREEZING FOOD

I don't know where I would be without my freezer. It is my own personal chef when things get a bit manic between work and football.

First things first: your freezer requires a little bit of love in terms of defrosting at least once a year. Investing in resealable and stackable containers in a variety of sizes is worth it. Freezer bags are also brilliant for vegetables, leftover bakes and organising items in one place. Here are some tips on freezing different types of food:

MEAT AND FISH
– Fresh: wrap in parchment and freeze individually.
– Cooked: allow to cool completely, then freeze in a resealable container or bag.

FRUIT AND VEGETABLES
– Fresh: peel, chop, place in resealable bags or containers and freeze. Berries should be placed on a lined tray with parchment first, frozen and then bagged to ensure they don't get stuck together.
– Cooked: allow to cool completely, then freeze in a resealable container or bag.

SOUP, BAKING, TREATS AND LEFTOVERS
– Allow to cool completely and freeze in resealable containers or bags.
– Cakes, including cheesecakes, should be frozen whole, cut into portions if required once semi-frozen, then individually wrapped and returned to the freezer. This is also the best method for dishes like lasagne or pies.

DEFROSTING FOOD

The ideal way to defrost food is in the fridge, stored in a suitable container. If using a microwave, only use the defrost function and follow the manufacturer's guidelines. Be especially careful with the defrost duration for meat as it can begin to cook. My advice is to take the item out of the freezer and allow it to defrost in the fridge overnight or during the day to ensure it is safe to use when you come home from work.

ZERO FOOD WASTE

Wasting food or anything in life is my pet peeve. That doesn't mean that you eat every morsel on your plate when eating out or that you eat gone-off food in your fridge. My best advice would be the following:

EATING OUT
– Ask to take home your leftover food or simply ask for a smaller portion.

FREEZE
– Divide into portions and freeze leftover dinners, soup, baked goods or fresh meat, fish, fruit and vegetables.

SMART SHOPPING
– Buy only what you need and get creative with what's in your fridge and freezer; some of my best recipes have come from having a bare fridge.

COMPOSTING
– Use a compost bin or start your own compost heap, which will reward you with compost for your garden. Another great way is to donate food waste to a nearby family member, neighbour or friend who has hungry animals that would happily eat your leftovers and peelings.

SHARE
– I haven't met anyone yet who doesn't appreciate free food! So why not bring in your leftovers to your colleagues or invite some friends or family over to enjoy your kitchen creations.

GROW IT YOURSELF

As a farmer's daughter and coming from a rural community, I'm very passionate about the land and the riches it delivers to our tables every day. At home, my mam always endeavoured to plant and grow vegetables in addition to our annual bounties of apples, raspberries and rhubarb from the garden. Eating imperfect apples and picking fruit was natural to me from a very young age.

Seasonal food is something that I think is getting lost in our day-to-day lives, as most fruit and vegetables are flown from all over the world to ensure we have year-round supplies. Everyone has experienced the sweet juicy taste of the first strawberries of summer in contrast to the dull strawberries available mid-winter.

By exploring the wonders of growing for yourself you will begin to develop an appreciation for all the hard work growers put in to ensure we have access to great ingredients. It is such a rewarding experience to see shoots and buds blossom into ripe produce ready for your table. You don't need an allotment or even a garden. All you need is light, moisture and somewhere to rest a pot. I have grown some of the best tomatoes from a small pot in a tiny courtyard in city-centre Dublin. Tomatoes are great to begin your growing adventures, as they take off with a little bit of feed, water and light.

Another great way to dip your toes in the water of growing is herbs – every supermarket sells pots of fresh herbs: pop them somewhere sunny indoors, keep them well hydrated and they will last for months.

The Grow It Yourself website (giy.ie) or your local garden centre are great places for more advice and to stock up on the necessary seeds, plants and equipment.

AN ATHLETE'S PLATE

'What do you eat before training, after training or a big match?' This is a question I commonly get asked by teammates, friends and through the blog. The simple answer is food – natural, unprocessed and seasonal are my three words of wisdom. All the recipes in this book are what I eat on a daily basis, although obviously the dessert chapter isn't for every day!

Nutritional advice for sportspeople and the general public is in a constant state of flux. The one consistent message available is the requirement for balanced energy sources to ensure you are adequately fuelling and repairing your body. Food group quantities and portion sizes vary significantly, depending on the level, duration and type of exercise involved.

A resource that I find very useful as a sportswoman is the Athlete Plate. This is a visual aid developed in collaboration between the United States Olympic Committee Sport Dietitians and the University of Colorado Sport Nutrition Graduate Program.

A choice of three plates is offered depending on your activity level to allow you fill your plate adequately with balanced food sources. These plates are useful not just for sportspeople but for anyone, as we all should eat off balanced plates.

EASY
– An easy day may contain a workout, tapering or a rest day without the need to load up with energy and nutrients for competition. This plate also applies to losing weight and athletes in sports requiring less energy.

MODERATE
– A moderate day may be one where you train twice a day, focusing on technical skill in one session and endurance or strength in another. This plate should be the baseline from which you adjust your plate up or down.

HARD/COMPETITION
– A hard day contains at least two workouts that are relatively hard or competitive. If your competition requires extra fuel from carbohydrates, use this plate to load up in the days before, throughout and after the event.

You should always listen to your body, how you are feeling, your energy levels and seek guidance from a qualified dietician.

EASY TRAINING / WEIGHT MANAGEMENT:

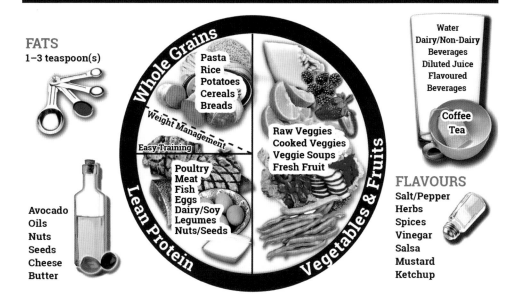

FATS
1–3 teaspoon(s)

Avocado
Oils
Nuts
Seeds
Cheese
Butter

Whole Grains
Pasta
Rice
Potatoes
Cereals
Breads

Weight Management
Easy Training

Lean Protein
Poultry
Meat
Fish
Eggs
Dairy/Soy
Legumes
Nuts/Seeds

Vegetables & Fruits
Raw Veggies
Cooked Veggies
Veggie Soups
Fresh Fruit

Water
Dairy/Non-Dairy
Beverages
Diluted Juice
Flavoured
Beverages

Coffee
Tea

FLAVOURS
Salt/Pepper
Herbs
Spices
Vinegar
Salsa
Mustard
Ketchup

MODERATE TRAINING:

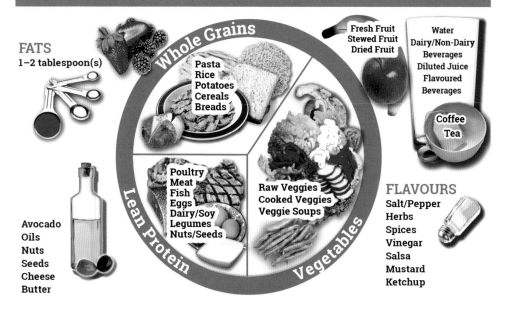

FATS
1–2 tablespoon(s)

Avocado
Oils
Nuts
Seeds
Cheese
Butter

Whole Grains
Pasta
Rice
Potatoes
Cereals
Breads

Lean Protein
Poultry
Meat
Fish
Eggs
Dairy/Soy
Legumes
Nuts/Seeds

Vegetables
Raw Veggies
Cooked Veggies
Veggie Soups

Fresh Fruit
Stewed Fruit
Dried Fruit

Water
Dairy/Non-Dairy
Beverages
Diluted Juice
Flavoured
Beverages

Coffee
Tea

FLAVOURS
Salt/Pepper
Herbs
Spices
Vinegar
Salsa
Mustard
Ketchup

HARD TRAINING:

FATS
2-3 tablespoons

Grains

Pasta
Rice
Potatoes
Cereals
Breads

Fresh Fruit
Stewed Fruit
Dried Fruit

Water
Dairy/Non-Dairy
Beverages
Diluted Juice
Flavoured
Beverages

Coffee
Tea

Lean Protein

Poultry
Meat
Fish
Eggs
Dairy/Soy
Legumes
Nuts/Seeds

Cooked Veggies
Veggie Soups
Raw Veggies

Vegetables

Avocado
Oils
Nuts
Seeds
Cheese
Butter

FLAVOURS

Salt/Pepper
Herbs
Spices
Vinegar
Salsa
Mustard
Ketchup

YOUR HEALTH IS YOUR WEALTH

HYDRATION

Did you know our bodies are made up of about 60 per cent water? Dehydration is a precursor to many ailments and underperformance in sport. I know it might sound unpleasant but keeping an eye on your urine colour is the easiest way to ensure you are well hydrated. Clear or light yellow is what you are looking for; anything else means you need to drink plenty of water.

EXERCISE

The only barrier to exercise is the one we create ourselves.

You can be as judicious as you want in the kitchen but ultimately you also need to move your body. As a physiotherapist I come across all types of patients on a daily basis from athletes with injuries, to elderly fallers, to those with chronic diseases. All of them have varying symptoms and issues but the common feature they all have is the need to exercise.

Exercise isn't a one-for-all fit. Some people require assistance to get up and move, while others need specific muscle and joint targeted rehabilitation programmes. Our bodies are designed to move but that movement is being reduced due to the advances in modern life. This reduction in daily movement is hampering our welfare and ultimately our health, shown by the rapidly growing levels of obesity and chronic disease worldwide.

Sitting for long periods in one spot, be it in work, traffic or in front of a screen, is not good for us. Movement allows our bodies to function efficiently and encourages communication, interaction and involvement with our surroundings. There are a million different ways to exercise – my favourite is in a group. A group setting is motivating, full of encouragement and ultimately fosters friendships as you all work towards the same goal.

On the other hand, walking is one of the easiest and cheapest forms of exercise. It's my favourite way to clear my head after a long day or a bad result in football. I urge you to find your favourite way to exercise – your body will thank you for it.

International research and guidelines recommend at least 30 minutes of moderate exercise a day for adults and 60 minutes of moderate to vigorous exercise a day for children – moderate exercise equates to an increased breathing and heart rate whilst still being able to continue a conversation comfortably.

THE BRIGHT SIDE OF LIFE

Sometimes we can get bogged down in the humdrum of everyday life and forget to relish the simple things. We should appreciate every day and keep a check on our mental health. When the going gets tough it is very easy to see the darkness in life, have a glass-half-empty mentality and point the finger at all around you.

A positive mentality from just one person is all that is required to cause a ripple effect amongst a group and evoke a sea change. We all have this power within.

Think of how many times you hear people mope over the weather – why not challenge their thoughts and change the conversation topic to something more positive. Immediately your mind will be refreshed. Another great way is to smile (even though this may be through gritted teeth). Smiling and laughing are infectious but often lacking in our lives, so smile and the world will smile back at you!

We only get one life and one body.
So nourish it, fuel it, challenge it, listen to it
and enjoy it.

KITCHEN ESSENTIALS

You don't need a big, spacious kitchen or the latest and fanciest equipment. All you need is a clean space, real food and the following equipment:

Knives

If you only buy one thing for your kitchen, invest in a good-quality chef's knife (20cm-blade) and a serrated or paring knife for preparing and peeling ingredients. They will last you a lifetime once you keep them clean, dry and sharp. The sharpening can be a bit tricky at times – most knives come with a sharpening steel; otherwise ask your local butcher to sharpen them for you. Serrated knives never need sharpening so they are a great buy.

Food Processor or Hand-held Stick Blender

It's worth investing in the best you can comfortably afford. I have a two-in-one processor and blender, which saves on space. Generally, the higher the strength, the smoother the results. Stick blenders are very affordable and useful for many things. Inserted directly into a saucepan or portable beaker, they are great for blending soups or smoothies whilst saving on washing-up!

Chopping Boards

Timber is my favourite as they don't stain and they last a lifetime. Boards that slide on your worktop are a nightmare so place a dampened paper towel underneath the board to keep in place.

Storage Containers

Reuse glass jars and bottles – simply sterilise them first by washing, then placing them in a warm oven until dry. Try to buy resealable containers made of glass, silicon or BPA-free plastic. Use these for storing food in the fridge or freezer, bringing meals on the go or simply having a more organised cupboard.

Patience, Perseverance and Practice

The Three Ps will see you through any kitchen disaster or sticky situation.

USING MY BOOK

A major aim of my recipes and blog is to make good food accessible and suitable for all. You will find recipes for everyone within these pages, so enjoy!

- If you are gluten or lactose intolerant, replace any regular flour with a gluten-free blend, plain oats and baking powder with gluten-free varieties and any dairy products with a lactose-free version.

- For all my vegetarian friends, remove the meat and substitute with a meat-free protein or increase the quantity of vegetables.

- All recipes include measurements using tsp (teaspoon) or tbsp (tablespoon). Consistently use the appropriately sized spoons in your cutlery drawer.

- Oat flour is simply oats blitzed in a food processor or blender until a flour-like substance is formed. It may contain some lumps, which is perfectly fine.

- Ingredient quality affects the flavour. I would encourage you to use native produce when you can and invest in the best-quality ingredients you can afford. Try to support independent suppliers and producers where possible, like your local butcher, fishmonger, baker and farmers' market.

- The majority of my recipe ingredients are available to purchase in your local supermarket. Spices, herbs and grains can be purchased in your local ethnic store where you will buy a year's supply for the same price as a tiny quantity in your supermarket. It is worth stocking up on these as they won't spoil in your cupboard.

- Don't be afraid to add your own twist or to mix and match ideas from my recipes. Recipes are ultimately inspiration and ideas that I hope will foster lots of creativity and happiness in your kitchen.

- Finally, read the recipe, organise your ingredients, re-read the recipe and then begin!

Happy cooking!

Sinéad

Breakfast

The Best Way to Start Your Day

Granola	30
Bircher Muesli	32
Cupcake Quiches	34
Quinoa and Oat Banana Bake	36
Bacon and Balsamic Roasted Tomato Flatbreads	38
Juices	40
Oat and Berry Recharger	42
Smoky Baked Beans with Bacon and Sourdough	44
Buckwheat Pancakes	46
Banana and Oat Pancakes	48
Carrot, Courgette and Corn Fritters	50
Crunchy Date and Seed Plum Pots	52

GRANOLA

This is my go-to breakfast and actually my first ever recipe on the blog. There is no better way to start the day than topping natural yoghurt and fresh fruit with this granola. Make a big batch at the start of the week and store in a glass jar.

The best thing about homemade granola is that you control the ingredients and most importantly the sugar content compared to regular cereals. This recipe certainly won't taste as sweet and gradually you can even eliminate the honey completely – you won't notice it's missing!

Makes 300g

1 tbsp honey

3 tbsp coconut oil, melted

10 tbsp oats (jumbo/porridge)

2 tbsp each of pumpkin, sunflower, poppy and sesame seeds

2 tbsp desiccated coconut

2 tbsp milled linseed

2 tbsp mixed nuts, chopped

1 tbsp flaked almonds

2 tbsp dried fruit (cranberries/raisins/ currants/apricots)

1 Preheat the oven to 200°C/180°C Fan/400°F and line a baking tray with parchment.

2 Whisk the honey and coconut oil together in a large mixing bowl until the honey is fully dissolved.

3 Add all the dry ingredients excluding the dried fruit into the bowl and stir through until well coated.

4 Spread the mixture evenly on the lined baking tray and place in the oven. Bake for 20 minutes, stirring regularly to ensure an even golden colour. Add the dried fruit just as the oats begin to turn golden.

5 Remove from the oven and allow to cool before storing in a large jar to be enjoyed every morning.

Handy hints!

- Make sure to keep a close eye on the granola as it cooks. It can easily burn; stirring the oats regularly will ensure it browns evenly.
- Customise the mixture of nuts, seeds and dried fruit to your liking – believe me, you can't go wrong!
- If you don't have an oven, fear not! Use a large frying pan or wok over a medium heat and follow the steps above.

BIRCHER MUESLI

If you aren't a great morning person, then here is the recipe for you. Prepare your breakfast the night before and simply enjoy straight from the fridge come morning.

Serves 2

80g oats (jumbo/porridge)
2 tbsp milled linseed
1 tbsp hemp or chia seeds
1 tbsp flaked almonds
1 tbsp raisins/dried cranberries/apricot
1 tsp ground cinnamon
Zest and juice of ½ a small orange
150ml milk (regular/nut/rice/oat/soya)
50ml water

1   Place all the dry ingredients in a bowl or portable food container.

2   Add the orange zest and juice along with the milk and water.

3   Stir well together and store in the fridge overnight (if you think the mix looks a little dry or you like a more gooey texture just add more milk or water).

4   Come morning, stir again to ensure it's well combined. Serve with orange segments and a dollop of natural or Greek yoghurt.

The milk and water volumes can be switched easily to all milk, water or a fruit juice of your liking. A mix of all three is nice too.

Apple and Cinnamon

Replace the orange zest and juice, dried fruit and flaked almonds with 1 grated small apple and 2 tsp ground cinnamon. Serve with apple slices, a dollop of natural or Greek yoghurt and a sprinkle of cinnamon.

CUPCAKE QUICHES

These quiches make a great brunch feast or are perfect as a fuss-free lunch. Simply make a big batch and keep in the freezer for when you need them.

If you are not a fish fan, then replace with ham, chicken or any other meat. You can also keep it vegetarian by simply increasing the vegetable quantities.

Makes 12 cupcakes

4 eggs
150ml milk
2 smoked mackerel fillets, flaked
10 cherry tomatoes, halved
2 spring onions, finely sliced
5 medium mushrooms, finely sliced
50g feta cheese, cubed
Freshly ground pepper
2 large handfuls kale/spinach,
   roughly chopped
2 tsp sweet chilli sauce (see page 86)

1 Preheat the oven to 200°C/180°C Fan/400°F and line a cupcake tray with silicone cases or grease each section with some oil.

2 Whisk the eggs and milk together in a large mixing bowl.

3 Add in the mackerel, tomatoes, spring onions, mushrooms and feta.

4 Season with some pepper and whisk all the ingredients together.

5 Evenly pour the mixture into the cases and bake in the oven for 30 minutes or until a skewer comes out clean.

6 Leave to cool in the cases and gently ease out onto a wire rack.

7 To serve: dry fry the kale or spinach over a medium heat until it begins to wilt (or use a microwave on high for 2 minutes), transfer to a plate and stack the cupcakes on top. Sprinkle over the sweet chilli sauce.

Variation

Pump up the protein by serving with a dollop of cottage cheese on top or sprinkle over a little dukkah (see page 85) for a spice infusion.

QUINOA AND OAT BANANA BAKE

Another one of my make-ahead breakfasts. I generally make this on a Sunday evening and then keep it fresh in the fridge. Simply reheat a portion in the morning and top with some Greek yoghurt and seeds. I love to have this in the depths of winter or the week of a big match.

Serves 5

85g quinoa
250ml water
3 tbsp nut butter
2 tbsp honey
1 egg
250ml milk (regular/oat/soy/nut)
3 bananas, sliced
50g walnuts, roughly chopped
1 tsp ground cinnamon
2 tbsp chia seeds
2 tbsp milled linseed
3 tbsp oats (jumbo/porridge)

1 Preheat the oven to 180°C/160°C Fan/350°F.
2 Place the quinoa and water in a large saucepan and gently bring to a boil with the lid on. Allow to boil for 2–3 minutes and then remove from the heat, leaving the lid on. The quinoa will continue to absorb all of the water.
3 Whisk together the nut butter and honey in a measuring jug until smooth. Continue to whisk as you add the egg and milk.
4 Add the banana and walnuts to the jug and stir together until the banana is well combined.
5 Pour the milk mixture with the cinnamon, seeds and oats over the cooked quinoa. Stir together until well combined.
6 Place the mixture into a loaf tin or ovenproof dish and bake in the oven for 60 minutes or until firm through.
7 If you're planning ahead for the week then allow it to cool, cover with parchment and store in the fridge. Reheat for 2 minutes in the microwave on high and serve with some yoghurt and seeds.

Handy hint!

This recipe is also a great way to use up leftover quinoa – just skip step 2 and use double the quantity, i.e. 170g cooked quinoa.

BACON AND BALSAMIC ROASTED TOMATO FLATBREADS

This dish is perfect for sharing so invite some friends over and tuck in! The flatbreads can be made in advance and frozen flat. If bacon isn't your dream start to the day, then why not grill some halloumi or vegetables.

Makes 5 flatbreads

For the flatbreads:
200g wholemeal flour
80g plain white flour
3 tsp baking powder
1 tsp salt
2 tbsp mixed herbs
240g Greek-style yoghurt
Coconut oil

For the toppings:
10 cherry tomatoes
1 tbsp balsamic vinegar
Guacamole (see page 87)
10 slices streaky smoked
    bacon, grillled
5 large handfuls salad leaves

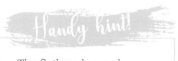

Handy hint!

The flatbreads are also delicious on their own, cut into triangles and dipped into hummus or soups.

1 Place all the dry flatbread ingredients in a large mixing bowl.
2 Create a well in the centre, add the yoghurt and stir together using your hands or a fork until a dough forms.
3 Turn the dough out onto a lightly floured surface and knead for about 5–10 minutes. Form the dough into a ball and place in a lightly oiled clean bowl. Cover with a tea towel and allow to rise in a warm place for at least 45 minutes. The dough is ready once it bounces back when pressed.
4 Whilst the dough is rising, preheat the oven to 120°C/100°C Fan/250°F. Place the tomatoes in an ovenproof dish and combine with the balsamic vinegar and 1 teaspoon of coconut oil. Slow roast in the oven for 1 hour.
5 Make the guacamole and place in the fridge until ready to serve.
6 When the dough has risen, literally punch it out on a clean surface and divide into 10 even balls. Use a rolling pin to roll each ball into a flatbread shape. Flip the dough over after each roll to ensure it doesn't stick to your worktop.
7 Place a grill or non-stick frying pan over a medium heat. Brush each flatbread with melted coconut oil and place on the pan. Bake each one until it begins to puff up, then turn over and cook on the opposite side.
8 To serve: spread 1 teaspoon of guacamole over each flatbread, then add the rocket, roasted tomatoes and bacon on top. Finish with another dollop of guacamole.

JUICES

I love a zingy wake-up call by gulping down a glass of green juice to kick-start my five-a-day. Juices and smoothies are a great way to squeeze some extra vegetables into your diet. Adding ginger helps to fuel your immune system from the inside out.

Each recipe makes 750ml of juice and will keep fresh in the fridge for 2–3 days.

GINGER BUG

1 head baby gem lettuce, roughly
   chopped
½ ripe avocado, cubed
Zest and juice of ½ lemon
Thumb-sized piece of fresh ginger,
   thinly sliced
2 tbsp fresh mint leaves, roughly chopped
250ml water

1 Place all the ingredients in a blender or juicer.
2 Set the blender to the highest setting until all the mix is reduced.
3 Give the mix a shake to ensure no lumps are left. You may need to add some more water at this stage if it is too lumpy.

THE FLU-FIGHTER

2 small apples, cored and cubed
Juice of 1 lemon
1 large carrot, de-stalked, peeled and
   cubed
2 medium-sized pre-cooked beetroot,
   cubed
Thumb-sized piece of fresh ginger,
   thinly sliced
250ml water

Variations

- Any leafy greens like spinach or chard can be used instead of kale or lettuce.
- Pear is a great substitute for apple.
- Half an avocado will instantly add a creamier texture.

GREEN-EYED MONSTER

3 celery sticks, finely sliced
Juice of 1 lemon
Thumb-sized piece of fresh ginger,
   thinly sliced
1 large apple, cored and cubed
5 large leaves kale, destalked and
   roughly chopped
½ cucumber, roughly cubed
300ml water or coconut water

Handy hint!

A hand-held stick blender works perfectly too, it just requires a little more work!

OAT AND BERRY RECHARGER

This smoothie is light and easy to digest whilst being super quick to prepare. I find smoothies are a perfect option for breakfast on the go or as a post-training recharger.

Recovery after tough exercise is vital for our muscles to repair and develop in the form of fluids, carbohydrate and protein. If I'm travelling some distance to training or have an early-morning session before work, I will blend the fruit and oats with a little water at home the night before, then buy some milk after training to mix through, ensuring it doesn't sour in my gear bag.

Any fresh or frozen berry combination works perfectly in this recipe!

Serves 1

40g oats
2 tbsp blueberries, fresh or frozen
½ medium apple, cubed
300ml milk (regular/nut/soy)

1 Place all the ingredients in a blender or portable beaker/measuring jug if using a hand-held blender.
2 Blend until smooth. Add some more milk or water if you find the consistency too thick.

Handy hint!

If your preference is to use protein powder, add one scoop of the powder with water instead of the milk.

Variation

Banana and Nut Butter
Use the above method, replacing the fruit with the following ingredients:
1 large banana, 2 tsp ground cinnamon and 1 tbsp nut butter (see page 88 for my Almond Butter recipe).

SMOKY BAKED BEANS WITH BACON AND SOURDOUGH

Baked beans get a bad rap, from keeping many students alive through college to being a key ingredient in a typical greasy fry.

Beans and lentils are a brilliant source of protein as they are easy to prepare and cheap to purchase. This recipe will banish any memories of your student days eating them straight from the tin and bring a warm glow to your morning.

Serves 4

Coconut oil
500g ripe vine tomatoes/1 x 400g tin
    chopped tomatoes
1 medium onion, diced
3 cloves garlic, minced
2 tbsp balsamic vinegar
3 bay leaves or 1 tsp dried mixed herbs
1 tsp honey
1 tsp paprika
2 x 400g tins cannellini/butter beans,
    drained and rinsed
4 slices sourdough bread
4 slices smoked/streaky bacon rashers
50g feta cheese, crumbled
Fresh parsley, roughly chopped

1 If using fresh tomatoes, roast them whole with 1 tsp coconut oil in a roasting tin at 200°C/180°C Fan/400°F for 30 minutes or until the skin blisters.

2 Over a medium heat, melt 1 teaspoon coconut oil in a large saucepan and sauté the onion and garlic until soft through. Add the tinned or roasted tomatoes, balsamic vinegar, bay leaves, honey and paprika. Bring to the boil and reduce to a simmer for 5 minutes.

3 Remove from the heat and blend with a stick blender until smooth.

4 Stir through the beans and return to a low heat until heated through.

5 Toast the sourdough and cook the bacon under the grill.

6 Stack the bacon onto the sourdough, spoon over the beans and finish with some crumbled feta and parsley.

BREAKFAST

PANCAKES

I adore pancakes in all shapes, sizes, flavours and, most importantly, at any time of the day or year! The banana and oat pancakes (see page 48) are my preference the morning of a match.

BUCKWHEAT
Makes 6 pancakes, serves 2

300ml regular or almond milk
1 tsp vanilla extract
125g buckwheat flour
½ tsp baking powder
Coconut oil

1 Place all the ingredients excluding the coconut oil in a bowl or jug and whisk until a smooth batter forms.
2 Allow to sit overnight or for at least 1 hour in the fridge.
3 Remove the batter from the fridge and give it another whisk to ensure no lumps of flour remain.
4 Heat 1 teaspoon of coconut oil on a non-stick pan over a medium heat. Add one ladle of the mixture, swirl the pan to get an even coating and cook for 3–5 minutes. Once little bubbles appear on top, flip over, cook through on the opposite side and remove from the heat.
5 Repeat with remaining pancake batter.
6 Serve with some yoghurt and berries.

Variation

For seriously fancy savoury pancakes, leave out the vanilla extract and serve with some smoked salmon, avocado and crème fraîche.

BREAKFAST

BANANA AND OAT
Makes 3 pancakes, serves 1

2 eggs

1 large banana, chopped

2 tbsp milled linseed

3 tbsp oats

100ml milk (any type)

Coconut oil

1   Whisk the eggs in a measuring jug.

2   Continue to whisk as you add the banana, linseed and oats until the banana is well combined.

3   Add the milk and whisk to combine fully.

4   Heat ½ teaspoon coconut oil on a non-stick frying pan over a medium heat. Pour in one third of the mixture, swirl the pan to get an even coating and cook for 2–4 minutes. Once little bubbles appear on top, flip over, cook through on the opposite side and remove from the heat.

5   Repeat with remaining pancake batter.

6   Serve with banana slices and nut butter.

Variation

The plum compote from page 52 is also great poured over the pancakes with a dollop of yoghurt.

CARROT, COURGETTE AND CORN FRITTERS

Fritters are a simple and tasty way to use up vegetables that are not at their best. This recipe is perfect for brunch or a midweek lunch as they freeze perfectly too.

Makes 6 medium fritters

2 eggs
2 tbsp milk
2 tbsp coconut flour/4 tbsp plain flour
1 carrot, grated
½ courgette, grated
1 x 225g tin corn, drained
½ red onion, finely diced
2 spring onions, finely sliced
Coconut oil
Green leaves

1 In a large mixing bowl, whisk together the eggs, milk and flour until it resembles a batter.
2 Add all the vegetables. Mix together until well combined.
3 Melt ½ teaspoon of coconut oil on a non-stick pan over a medium heat. Place a heaped tablespoon of the mixture on the pan and flatten into a round shape.
4 Allow to cook fully before flipping over. Once cooked, remove from pan and place on a parchment-lined tray in the oven on a low heat.
5 Repeat with the remaining mixture.
6 Serve on a bed of green leaves. Tomato relish or guacamole (see page 87) are great on the side too.

Variation

Turn your fritters into burgers by doubling the recipe quantity and frying 2 tbsp of the mixture at a time to create a generous-sized burger. Cook as before and serve in a pitta, bun burger or alongside a salad.

CRUNCHY DATE AND SEED PLUM POTS

These little beauties are perfect for mixing up your breakfast routine with little effort. They are also a quick snack or dessert option. When plums aren't in season, use apples, pears, apricots, peaches or nectarines.

Serves 5

500g Greek-style yoghurt

Plum Compote

6 plums, halved and stoned
1 tsp honey
100ml water
2 small apples, peeled, cored and halved

Date and Seed Crunch

2 tbsp black sesame seeds
2 tbsp white sesame seeds
1 tbsp poppy seeds
2 tbsp brown linseed
2 tbsp raw cacao nibs
4 dates, stoned and finely diced
1 tbsp dried apricot, finely diced
2 tbsp buckwheat groats
1 tbsp desiccated coconut

For the plum compote:

1 Place the plums, honey and water in a small saucepan with the lid on.
2 Bring to the boil and reduce to a simmer for 5 minutes.
3 Add the apple halves, reduce to the lowest heat and continue to simmer until the apple is cooked through and beginning to break up.
4 Remove from the heat and allow to cool.
5 Store in an airtight jar in the fridge once cooled.

For the date and seed crunch:

1 Place all the ingredients together in a jar and shake to mix.
2 Store in an airtight jar and keep in a cool, dark place.

To assemble:

1 Spoon the yoghurt into a short glass or small bowl.
2 Top with a tablespoon of plum compote and a sprinkle of the seed crunch.

Baking

Recipes Guaranteed to Make You Friends

Oat and Seed Yoghurt Loaf	56
Seeded Spelt Scones	58
Fluffy Oat Scones	60
Raspberry and Almond Coins	62
Apricot and Pecan Flapjacks	64
Fruit and Nut Dark Chocolate Oaties	66
Berry and Oat Muffins	68
Dark Chocolate and Walnut Banana Bread	70
Carrot Cake with Yoghurt Icing	72
Spelt Babhka Rolls	74
Cashew and Dark Chocolate Bites	76

OAT AND SEED YOGHURT LOAF

This loaf is made in minutes and it's suitable for all. Simply use gluten-free oats and lactose-free yoghurt as required. I love a slice of this loaf with a bowl of soup at lunchtime.

Makes 1 loaf

300g oats

1 tbsp pumpkin seeds

1 tbsp sunflower seeds

2 tbsp milled linseed

2 tsp bread soda

500g natural yoghurt

1 Preheat the oven to 200°C/180°C Fan/400°F and line a loaf tin with oil or parchment.

2 Place all the dry ingredients in a large mixing bowl.

3 Add the yoghurt and mix thoroughly.

4 Place the oat mix into the loaf tin. Sprinkle some more oats and seeds on top.

5 Bake for 40 minutes or until a knife comes out clean.

6 Remove from the tin and allow to cool on a wire rack.

Handy hint!

To freeze, slice the baked and cooled loaf into thirds or individual slices, wrap in parchment and place in the freezer.

Variation

Mediterranean Style Loaf

Replace the pumpkin and sunflower seeds with 6 chopped sun-dried tomatoes, 2 tbsp fennel seeds, 1 tbsp tomato puree and 2 tbsp extra-virgin olive oil.

SEEDED SPELT SCONES

These are my dad's favourites! He loves nothing more than taking a break between jobs down on the farm with a flask of tea and one of these scones, topped with my mam's famous homemade raspberry jam. My favourite topping is homemade almond butter (see page 88) and sliced banana.

Makes 15

200g jumbo oats
2 tbsp rapeseed oil
500ml buttermilk
200g spelt wholemeal flour
3 tbsp milled linseed
1 heaped tsp bread soda
1 tbsp pumpkin seeds
1 tbsp sunflower seeds
1 tbsp sesame seeds
½ tsp salt
1 egg yolk
Dash of milk

1 Place the oats in a large mixing bowl and stir through the oil and 300ml of the buttermilk. Cover and place in the fridge for at least 2 hours.

2 Preheat the oven to 190°C/170°C Fan/375°F. Grease and line two baking trays with parchment.

3 Add the flour, linseed, bread soda, seeds and salt to the oats and mix together whilst gradually adding the remaining buttermilk until it forms a loose dough.

4 Turn the dough out onto a lightly floured surface and evenly flatten to about 1 inch thick.

5 Cut into squares using a knife and place onto the baking trays.

6 Whisk the egg yolk with a dash of milk and brush over each scone before sprinkling with some sesame seeds.

7 Bake in the oven for 20 minutes or until golden brown.

8 Remove from the oven and allow to cool on a wire rack.

Variation

Berry Scones
Replace the pumpkin, sunflower and sesame seeds with 2 tbsp fresh or frozen berries. Add to the scone mix just after the flour.

FLUFFY OAT SCONES

These scones are beautiful fresh from the oven and slathered with some jam or nut butter. The oat flour creates a nice light and fluffy texture.

My favourite additions to these scones are raisins or fresh pear rolled in cinnamon. Seeds or dried fruit are other great combinations.

Makes 20

300g oat flour
260g wholemeal flour
2 tsp baking powder
1 tsp bread soda
1 tsp salt
220g unsalted butter, chilled and cubed
300g porridge oats
130g raisins or 2 tbsp ground cinnamon and 2 pears, peeled, cored and cubed
480ml buttermilk
1 egg, beaten

1 Preheat the oven to 190°C/170°C Fan/375°F and line two large baking trays with parchment.
2 Mix together the flours, baking powder, baking soda and salt in a large bowl.
3 Rub the butter into the flour mix with your fingertips until it resembles breadcrumbs.
4 Add the oats and raisins. Stir to distribute. evenly. If using cinnamon and pear, roll the pear in the cinnamon before adding to the scone mix.
5 Add the buttermilk and stir with a fork until it gathers into a rough ball.
6 Sprinkle a clean worktop with flour and place the dough on top. Knead the dough gently to bring it all together into a ball.
7 Roll out the dough with a floured rolling pin into a 1-inch-thick rectangle.
8 Cut into squares and place on the baking tray.
9 Brush each scone with the beaten egg.
10 Bake in the oven for 25 minutes or until golden.

BAKING

RASPBERRY AND ALMOND COINS

These are small but mighty raspberry delights, perfect with a hot drink at the end of a meal or as a mid-morning treat.

Makes 20

150g ground almonds
1 egg, beaten
50g coconut oil, melted
3 tbsp honey
100g raspberry jam

1 Mix together the almonds, egg, coconut oil and honey with a fork until a dough ball is formed.
2 Cover with parchment and place in the fridge to chill for at least an hour.
3 Preheat the oven to 180°C/160°C Fan/350°F and line a baking tray with parchment.
4 Remove the dough from the fridge and roll out between two sheets of parchment until a 1-inch-thick rectangle is formed.
5 Use a cookie cutter to cut out coin-shaped cookies and place onto the lined tray.
6 Press down the centre of each cookie with your thumb to form a small well. Spoon the jam into each well.
7 Bake in the oven for 10–12 minutes or until golden.
8 Allow to cool on the tray before removing. Store in an airtight container.

Variations

- Dark Chocolate
  No need to create a well in each coin before baking. Melt 50g dark chocolate and dip half of each cooled coin in the chocolate. Allow to dry on parchment.
- Almond
  No need to create a well in each coin before baking. Simply place a flaked almond in the centre of each cookie instead of the jam.

APRICOT AND PECAN FLAPJACKS

These flapjacks are very low in sugar and perfect for snacking whilst out exploring the great outdoors. Replace the apricots and pecans with any dried fruit or nuts of your choice.

Makes 12

55g butter

2 tbsp honey

3 tbsp tahini/nut butter

55g oat flour

140g jumbo oats

1 tsp baking powder

25g dried cranberries

55g dried apricots, chopped

25g pecans, chopped

1 egg white

Dash of milk

1   Preheat the oven to 200°C/180°C Fan/400°F and line a 21cm square baking tray with parchment.

2   Place the butter, honey and tahini in a small saucepan and gently melt together over a low heat until a runny mixture is formed.

3   Place all the dry ingredients (reserving a teaspoon of the dried fruit and pecans) in a large mixing bowl and stir through the melted ingredients until well combined.

4   Whisk the egg white with a dash of milk and stir through the oat mix.

5   Pour into the lined baking tray and flatten with the back of a spoon.

6   Sprinkle over the remaining dried fruit and pecans. Bake in the oven for 20 minutes or until golden brown.

7   Allow to cool in the tin before removing and cutting into bars.

8   Store in an airtight container.

FRUIT AND NUT DARK CHOCOLATE OATIES

Cookies were one of the first things I learnt to bake and I even sold them to my classmates in primary school. I would eagerly await the cookies from our AGA cooker at home, standing guard beside them as they cooled and then devouring one with a glass of milk.

These oaties are a variation of those famous cookies with oats added and are equally as delicious.

Makes 12

1 egg
2 tbsp honey
100g butter, melted
1½ tsp vanilla extract
100g oat flour
100g jumbo oats
2 tbsp hazelnuts, halved
2 tbsp dried cranberries/raisins
1 tsp bread soda
2 tsp boiling hot water
25g dark chocolate
1 tsp coconut oil

1 Preheat the oven to 180°C/160°C Fan/350°F and line two baking trays with parchment.

2 In a large bowl, whisk the egg, honey, butter and vanilla extract well together. Add the oat flour, jumbo oats, nuts and dried fruit, stirring well to combine.

3 In a small bowl, mix the baking soda and hot water together until dissolved. Add to the oat mix and combine.

4 Spoon large tablespoons of the cookie mix onto the prepared trays and flatten with the back of the spoon.

5 Bake for 15–20 minutes or until golden.

6 Remove from the oven and allow to cool on a wire rack.

7 As the cookies cool, melt the dark chocolate in a heatproof bowl over a simmering pot of water. Once melted, remove from the heat and stir through the coconut oil until well combined.

8 Drizzle the dark chocolate over the cooled cookies.

9 Store in an airtight container or freeze.

BERRY AND OAT MUFFINS

These low-sugar muffins are bursting with slow-release carbohydrates and berry goodness. This makes them ideal for a quick breakfast or as a snack.

Use whatever berries you like, add some chopped nuts or chunks of dark or white chocolate ... the possibilities are endless! The muffins will stay fresh for at least four days in an airtight container or you can freeze them, if any survive that long!

Makes 10

170g oat flour

55g desiccated coconut

1½ tsp baking powder

Pinch of salt

110g butter, softened

2 tbsp honey

1 egg

2 overripe bananas

½ tsp vanilla extract

4 tbsp natural yoghurt

4 tbsp fresh or frozen berries (blueberries and raspberries are my favourite)

Coconut flakes

1 Preheat the oven to 200°C/180°C Fan/400°F and either oil or line a muffin tray with cases.

2 Mix the oat flour with the desiccated coconut, baking powder and salt in one bowl.

3 In a separate large mixing bowl, using a hand-held beater, cream the butter and honey together until light and fluffy. Beat through the egg.

4 Mash the bananas and vanilla extract together before adding to the butter mix. Stir through the flour mix until well combined.

5 Finally add the yoghurt and berries until well combined.

6 Spoon the muffin batter evenly amongst the muffin cases, top with some fresh oats and coconut flakes before placing in the oven for 15–20 minutes until golden brown or a skewer comes out clean.

Handy hint!

After you add the egg, the mix might look curdled. You haven't gone wrong, I promise!

DARK CHOCOLATE AND WALNUT BANANA BREAD

Banana bread is a great way to use up overripe bananas; dark chocolate and walnut make tasty additions. Be sure to use the ripest bananas you have as they make the best loaves.

Makes 1 loaf

30g coconut flour/125g plain flour
80g ground almonds
50g oat flour
1 tsp baking powder
1 tsp ground cinnamon
Pinch of salt
3 tbsp coconut oil, solid
2 tbsp honey
2 tbsp nut butter
3 eggs, beaten
3 overripe bananas, mashed
25g dark chocolate, chopped
   into little chunks
30g walnuts, roughly chopped

1 Preheat the oven to 200°C/180°C Fan/400°F and line a loaf tin with oil or parchment.
2 Place all the dry ingredients (excluding the chocolate and walnuts) into a large mixing bowl.
3 Melt the coconut oil in a small saucepan.
4 Once melted, stir through the honey and nut butter until well combined.
5 Add the eggs and mashed bananas to the dry ingredients and stir well to combine.
6 Pour in the melted ingredients and stir again to combine.
7 Stir through the chocolate and walnuts, saving a teaspoon of each to scatter over the top.
8 Transfer the dough to the prepared loaf tin and sprinkle over the saved chocolate and walnuts. Bake in the oven for 35–40 minutes or until a skewer comes out clean.
9 Cut into slices and freeze or store whole in an airtight container for 5 days.

Handy hint!

Freeze overripe bananas to ensure you have a stock for when required. Place the bananas whole and unpeeled in the freezer and defrost slightly at room temperature before using.

CARROT CAKE WITH YOGHURT ICING

Carrot cake is possibly my favourite cake; however, every time I make it I tweak the recipe another little bit. This version is gluten-free and very low in sugar.

The yoghurt icing may appear initially quite runny. Allow it to settle and thicken in the fridge before spreading on top. The cake is best kept fresh in the fridge for up to 5 days in an airtight container.

Serves 12

3 eggs
Zest of 1 small orange
60ml extra-virgin olive oil
1 ripe banana, mashed
1 tbsp honey
100g oat flour
100g desiccated coconut
100g ground almonds
2 tsp ground cinnamon
2 tsp baking powder
300g carrots, grated
50g walnuts, roughly chopped

For the icing:
3 tbsp Greek yoghurt
5 tbsp crème fraîche
1 tbsp honey
5 walnuts, roughly chopped

1 Preheat the oven to 180°C/160°C Fan/350°F. Line a 21cm square baking tin with parchment.
2 Whisk the eggs, orange zest, oil, mashed banana and honey together in a large bowl.
3 Stir in the oat flour, coconut, almonds, cinnamon and baking powder.
4 Add the grated carrot and chopped walnuts and stir until well combined.
5 Press the mixture down in the baking tin and bake in the oven for 40 minutes or until a skewer comes out clean.
6 Allow the carrot cake to cool in the tin before transferring to a wire rack.
7 For the icing: whisk the yoghurt, crème fraîche and honey together. Place in the fridge until required.
8 When the cake is fully cooled, add the icing and sprinkle the chopped nuts on top.

 Handy hint!

This carrot cake can also be baked in a loaf tin. Follow the steps and baking time as above.

SPELT BABHKA ROLLS

Babhka is traditionally a sweet bread similar to a brioche. Instead of a loaf, I've created little rolls, which are a perfect portion size.

This recipe is one of my favourites. The comforting smell of cinnamon as these bake is just delicious. I generally mix things up and make half a batch with cinnamon and pecan and the other half with dark chocolate and hazelnut.

Makes 12

500g spelt flour
1 tsp salt
50g brown sugar
110g butter, softened
2 tbsp coconut oil
210ml milk
1 tsp dried fast-action yeast
1 egg, beaten
1 additional egg yolk
Dash of milk

For the filling:
Cinnamon and Pecan
4 tbsp ground cinnamon
150g butter, softened
1 tbsp honey
3 tbsp pecans, chopped

Dark Chocolate and Hazelnut
100g dark chocolate
2 tsp coconut oil
3 tbsp hazelnuts, toasted
  and chopped

1 Line and grease a circular baking tray or shallow cake tin.

2 In a large mixing bowl, stir together the flour, salt and sugar. Rub in the softened butter and coconut oil with your fingertips until it resembles breadcrumbs.

3 Gently heat the milk in a measuring jug just to take the chill off, sprinkle in the yeast, stir and allow to dissolve fully.

4 Create a well in the flour, pour in the milk and add the beaten egg. Combine with your hands or a spatula until a dough forms.

5 Transfer the dough to a clean surface and knead for at least 10–15 minutes by hand. The dough will be quite sticky initially but will come together to form a smooth, supple dough. Place the dough in an oiled bowl, cover with a damp tea towel and allow to prove at room temperature for 60–90 minutes (the dough should bounce back when pressed down with your thumb).

6 For the filling:

   Cinnamon and Pecan – With an electric hand-held mixer or stand mixer, beat together the cinnamon, butter and honey until soft and fluffy.

   Dark Chocolate and Hazelnut – Melt the chocolate in a heatproof bowl over a pan of simmering water, then stir through the coconut oil to form a shiny, supple liquid.

7 Once the dough has proved, pre-heat the oven to 190°C/170°C Fan/375°F. Place the dough on a lightly floured work surface and literally punch it out. Using a lightly floured rolling pin, roll out the dough into a 1-inch-thick rectangle. Turn the dough over after each roll to prevent it sticking to your work surface.

8 Evenly spread the cinnamon or chocolate mix on top and sprinkle with ¾ of the chopped nuts.

9 Start with the longest edge and roll the dough into a Swiss-roll shape. Using a sharp knife, cut it into 2-inch-thick slices.

10 Place the slices onto the prepared baking tray and sprinkle over the remaining chopped nuts. Whisk the egg yolk with a dash of milk and brush over the rolls.

11 Bake for 35–40 minutes or until a skewer comes out clean. Transfer to a wire rack and cool.

Handy hints!

- If using a combination of fillings, use half the quantities of each filling.
- Replace spelt flour with strong white flour or make a combination of 50:50 spelt to strong flour. Wholemeal varieties can also be used to create a darker and drier dough. When working with wholemeal I would advise adding some percentage of white flour.
- Plan ahead and allow the dough to prove overnight in the fridge, removing 90 minutes before using to allow it return to room temperature (it should bounce back once pressed down), before filling and baking as described. Or fill, cut into rolls and place in the fridge, again removing 90 minutes before baking.

CASHEW AND DARK CHOCOLATE BITES

Would you ever guess that butter beans are the base of these moreish bites? Butter beans replace flour, resulting in the most delicious, soft and delicate treats. These are some of my most requested goodies to bring into work, so I promise they won't disappoint!

Makes 12

100g cashews, soaked for 3 hours

1 x 400g tin butter beans, drained and rinsed

4 tbsp honey or maple syrup

100g ground almonds

½ tsp bread soda

2 eggs

2 tsp vanilla extract

75g unsalted butter, softened

100g dark chocolate, chopped into chunks

1 Preheat the oven to 190°C/170°C Fan/375°F.

2 Drain and rinse the soaked cashews, place on a baking tray and bake in the oven for 7 minutes whilst the oven heats up. Line a 21cm square baking tin with parchment.

3 With a food processor or electric hand-held beater (if using an electric beater, mash or blend the beans first), blitz all the ingredients except the cashews and chocolate together until smooth.

4 Stir through 75g cashews and 80g dark chocolate chunks.

5 Pour into the tin and scatter the remaining cashews and dark chocolate over the top.

6 Bake in the oven for 30 minutes or until a skewer comes out clean.

7 Leave to cool in the tin, remove and cut into bites.

Variation

White Chocolate and Raspberry
Replace the dark chocolate with white and replace half the cashews with fresh or frozen raspberries.

Tasty Extras

The Hidden Gems in My Cupboard

Hummus   80

Pesto   82

Dukkah   85

Sweet Chilli Sauce   86

Frenchie Dressing   86

Creamy Tahini Dressing   87

Guacamole   87

Homemade Nut Butter   88

HUMMUS

The possibilities are endless with hummus. You can use all sorts of pulses, vegetables and spices to give you a different variation every day. I find hummus great as a snack with some vegetable sticks or as a dip with toasted sourdough for a simple starter.

Using pre-soaked and cooked dried pulses results in a creamier consistency but tinned pulses still make great hummus and I use them all the time. If using dried chickpeas or butterbeans, halve the cooked weight (i.e. 200g dried will result in 400g cooked). Soak the dried pulses for at least 8 hours fully covered in water, drain and cover again with water. Bring to a boil, cover and simmer for 2 hours or until the pulses are soft through when squeezed. Remember to retain the juice from both the cooked and tinned pulses.

Each recipe will make enough to serve 8 people, with a serving being about 4 tablespoons. I also generally freeze portion-sized batches in small pots and then allow to defrost in the fridge before eating.

Here are four of my favourite hummus recipes:

PARMESAN AND GARLIC

1 x 400g tin chickpeas, drained and rinsed
3 tbsp retained chickpea juice
2 cloves of garlic, minced
2 tbsp tahini
2 tsp ground cumin
1 tbsp parmesan, grated
4 tbsp extra-virgin olive oil

1 Place all the ingredients with 2 tablespoons of the oil in a food processor and blend until smooth.
2 Gradually add the remaining oil until you reach your preferred texture.

BEETROOT AND MINT

1 x 400g tin butter beans, drained and rinsed
300g cooked beetroot, cubed
2 tbsp fresh mint leaves, roughly chopped
50g walnuts
1 tbsp fresh lemon juice

1 Place the beans, beetroot and mint in a food processor. Blitz until a smooth purée is formed.
2 Add the walnuts and lemon juice. Blitz again until fully combined – the walnuts should still be a little bit crunchy.

TASTY EXTRAS

ROAST RED PEPPER AND SMOKED PAPRIKA

1 tbsp coconut oil

2 red peppers, de-seeded and halved

2 cloves garlic

1 x 400g tin chickpeas, drained and rinsed

3 tbsp retained chickpea juice

½ red chilli, de-seeded and finely chopped

2 tbsp lemon juice

3 tbsp tahini

2 tbsp smoked paprika

1 tsp ground cumin

1 Preheat the oven to 200°C/180°C Fan/400°F and melt the coconut oil in a large roasting tray.

2 Mix the peppers and garlic through the oil and roast in the oven for 20 minutes or until the skin blisters.

3 Once the peppers and garlic are roasted, squeeze the soft centre of the garlic out of the skin and discard the skin. Add to a food processor or blender with the remaining ingredients and blitz until smooth.

ROAST CARROT AND GARLIC

1 tsp coconut oil

4 large carrots, peeled and cubed

2 cloves garlic

1 tsp ground cumin

1 tsp ground coriander

1 tsp ground turmeric

1 x 400g tin chickpeas, drained and rinsed

3 tbsp retained chickpea juice

2 tbsp tahini

1 tbsp lemon juice

4 tbsp extra-virgin olive oil

1 Preheat the oven to 200°C/180°C Fan/400°F. Melt the coconut oil in a large roasting tray.

2 Add the carrots and garlic to the oil with the spices. Thoroughly mix together and roast in the oven for 20 minutes or until soft through.

3 Once the carrots and garlic are roasted, squeeze the soft centre of the garlic out of the skin and discard the skin.

4 Place all the ingredients with 2 tablespoons of oil in a food processor or blender. Continue to blend, slowly adding the remaining oil until it forms a smooth consistency (add more oil or water if you feel it is too dry).

PESTO

Pesto is such a versatile item to have in your fridge. It can instantly transform any dish. It is great stirred through pasta, steamed julienned or spiralised vegetables, or to replace butter in a sandwich.

I personally love it spread on thick slices of sourdough, toasted in the oven and topped with cottage cheese and tomatoes for some real comfort food.

Pesto is traditionally made with garlic, pine nuts, parmesan, basil and olive oil. The quality of olive oil does make a difference so try using the best you can comfortably afford. I love to play around with different flavours and ingredients so I've replaced the pine nuts with other ingredients but you can easily make all of the recipes with the traditional ingredients too.

The pesto will keep fresh in the fridge under an extra layer of olive oil for at least two weeks in an airtight jar.

CORIANDER, CASHEW AND WALNUT

50g cashews

50g walnuts

100ml extra virgin olive oil

2 cloves garlic

50g fresh coriander including the stalks

25g parmesan, grated

1 tbsp fresh lemon juice

1 Simply add all the ingredients with half the oil to a food processor and blitz until smooth.

2 Add the remaining oil little by little until you get a suitable texture, tasting as you go.

NETTLE AND PARMESAN

Ensure you pick young nettles that look much smaller and a lighter green than the bigger, older ones. Always wear gloves or wrap your hand in a plastic bag to prevent those nasty nettle stings. I promise the pesto doesn't sting!

25g freshly picked nettle tops
2 cloves garlic
25g ground almonds
140ml extra virgin olive oil
25g parmesan, grated

1 De-stalk the nettle tops and lightly rinse.
2 Strain the nettles and squeeze any excess water off.
3 Add the garlic, ground almonds and 3 tablespoons of olive oil to a food processor and gently pulse until they form a paste.
4 Continue to pulse, adding the nettles, parmesan and 1 tablespoon at a time of the remaining oil until it all combines into a pesto.

BASIL AND SUNFLOWER SEEDS

25g sunflower seeds
25g fresh basil leaves and stalks
1 tbsp fresh lemon juice
1 clove garlic
10g parmesan, grated
75ml extra-virgin olive oil

1 Toast the sunflower seeds on a dry pan over a medium heat until they begin to pop.
2 Add the toasted seeds, basil, lemon juice, garlic, parmesan and 2 tablespoon of oil to a food processor and blitz until the seeds have broken down considerably.
3 Continue to blitz as you slowly add the remaining oil. Add more oil if it is too dry.

Handy hint!

Sterilised jars are best for storing pesto, jams, chutneys or hummus.
Thoroughly wash a glass jar, then place in a hot oven until dry.

DUKKAH

I am obsessed with dukkah – it's my spicy fairy dust. Dukkah originates in Middle Eastern cooking and is typically served as a dip with bread and oil.

I tend to sprinkle it over any dish or salad to add a little bit of oomph. I can even be found eating it straight off the spoon or spreading it with tahini over a slice of bread as a snack.

Makes 1 jar

70g hazelnuts
1 tbsp sunflower seeds
1 tbsp pumpkin seeds
1 tsp fennel seeds
1 tbsp cumin seeds
1 tbsp white peppercorns
3 tbsp coriander seeds
1½ tbsp sesame seeds
½ tsp nigella seeds
1 tsp paprika
Zest of ½ lemon
2 tsp sea salt

1 Toast the hazelnuts in the oven at 180°C/160°C Fan/ 350°F until the skin begins to loosen. Remove from the oven and allow to cool.

2 Toast the sunflower and pumpkin seeds in the oven separately until they begin to pop, then remove to cool.

3 Heat a dry pan over a medium heat until you begin to see heat rise. Add the fennel seeds and toast for 30 seconds. Add the cumin seeds and toast together for a further 30 seconds or until they begin to pop. Remove from the pan and allow to cool.

4 Toast the white peppercorns in the same way for 30 seconds or until they begin to pop, then transfer to a separate bowl.

5 Cook the coriander seeds for up to 1 minute or until they begin to pop, then transfer to a separate bowl.

6 Reduce the heat to low and toast the sesame and nigella seeds until the sesame seeds become an even golden colour, then remove from the pan.

7 Using a pestle and mortar or tall mug and rolling pin, crush the hazelnuts into a coarse pulp. Add to a large bowl.

8 Repeat with the sunflower and pumpkin seeds before adding to the hazelnuts.

9 Lightly crush the fennel and cumin seeds. Repeat with the coriander seeds and peppercorns.

10 Mix all the crushed seeds and nuts together with the remaining ingredients and store in an airtight jar.

SWEET CHILLI SAUCE

You just can't compare the bought variation of this sauce to making your own. It will keep fresh in an airtight jar stored in a cool, dry place for at least one year. It is a great addition to your cupboard to use as a dipping sauce or as a base for stir-fries. It also makes a nice present to a foodie friend.

Makes 750ml

1 large red pepper, finely chopped
1 red chilli, de-seeded
 and finely chopped
100g caster sugar
100ml water
100ml rice wine vinegar

1. Place all the ingredients in a saucepan and bring to the boil. Reduce to a simmer and continue to cook for at least 20–30 minutes until the peppers are soft through.
2. Transfer to a large jug and blend using a hand-held blender to your preferred consistency.
3. Store in an airtight jar.

Handy hint!

As you know, chillies can be very spicy, but even more so they can burn. When working with chillies, DON'T rub your eyes! If it does unfortunately happen, rinse your eye with cold running water.

FRENCHIE DRESSING

This dressing is my all-time favourite; it works well with any salad and keeps fresh in the fridge for at least one month. Whip up a batch and you'll always have a tasty dressing to hand.

Makes 300ml

2 cloves garlic, minced
2 tbsp lemon juice
1 tsp freshly ground pepper
5 tbsp extra-virgin olive oil
5 tbsp sesame oil
2 tbsp apple cider vinegar
2 tbsp Dijon mustard
1 tbsp honey

1. Add all the ingredients to a jar, put on the lid and shake until well combined.
2. Taste and season with more pepper, honey or lemon juice as required.
3. Store in the fridge.

CREAMY TAHINI DRESSING

A simple dressing that takes seconds to make and is perfect drizzled over roasted vegetables, any salad or with a burger or falafel.

Serves 5

2 tbsp tahini
3 tbsp water
1 tbsp lemon juice

1   Whisk all the ingredients together in a small bowl until smooth.
2   If storing in the fridge, it will last a few days. Whisk again before serving if it begins to harden a little.

GUACAMOLE

Who doesn't love avocados and especially guacamole? Add it to your salad instead of dressing, top a baked potato with it for a quick meal or serve it as a side with any or all of your meals!

Serves 5

1 ripe avocado
Juice of 1 lime
½ red onion, diced
6 cherry tomatoes, quartered
1 tbsp fresh coriander, finely chopped
Pinch of sea salt

1   In a large bowl, mash the avocado with the lime juice. It doesn't have to be perfectly smooth, some lumps are good.
2   With a fork, stir through all the remaining ingredients.
3   Cover and store in the fridge until ready to serve.

HOMEMADE NUT BUTTER

Like a lot of people I LOVE nut butter but there is a huge range of quality and ingredients in shop-bought varieties.

By making your own you can control exactly what goes in, mix and match your favourite flavours and save a few pennies along the way. All you need to make your own at home is a high-strength blender or food processor and a sterile glass jar. My favourite is almond butter but substitute in your favourite nuts.

Nut butter is a great way to add some protein to your day but it can be addictive so watch your portion sizes – 2 tablespoons equals one portion.

Makes 600g

600g almonds
Pinch of salt

1 Preheat the oven to 200°C/180°C Fan/400°F and place the almonds on a large baking tray.
2 Roast for 20 minutes until they begin to crisp and turn a darker shade.
3 Place the roasted almonds in a food processor or blender and blitz on a medium speed until you get a coarse breadcrumb texture.
4 Continue to blitz, gradually increasing the speed until the natural oils of the almonds are released and a paste begins to form. This may take up to 20 minutes depending on the strength of your food processor or blender. You will also need to stop your machine and scrape down the sides regularly.
5 Add the salt and blitz again on full speed for another few minutes to ensure a smooth butter is formed.
6 Pour into a sterile glass jar and store in a cool, dry place.

Handy hint!

For Crunchy Nut Butter
Reserve 4 tbsp of the nuts after they have formed a coarse crushed mix. Stir through the smooth nut butter at the end.

Variation

Add even more flavour to your nut butter by choosing one of these extras:
• 4 tbsp melted coconut oil
• 1 tsp vanilla essence
• 2 tsp ground cinnamon
• 1 tbsp raw cacao

Soups

Comfort in a Bowl

Roast Root Vegetable and Coriander Soup	92
Mushroom and Fennel Soup	94
Pea, Spinach and Smoked Bacon Soup	96
Spiced Butternut Squash Soup	98
Creamy Broccoli and Cashew Soup	100
Roast Tomato and Red Pepper Soup	102
Beetroot and Carrot Soup	104
Creamy Roast Cauliflower Soup	106

ROAST ROOT VEGETABLE AND CORIANDER SOUP

I always find there are a few carrots, parsnips, turnip or sweet potatoes rolling around in the bottom of my vegetable drawer looking a little worse for wear. By simply roasting with some spices, you get the best flavour from not the prettiest looking vegetables.

Serves 6

Coconut oil
2 tsp ground coriander
1 tsp ground cumin
6 sprigs fresh rosemary or
   1 tsp dried rosemary
½ medium sweet potato, peeled and cubed
2 large carrots, peeled and cubed
2 medium parsnips, peeled and cubed
½ medium turnip, peeled and cubed
3 cloves of garlic, minced
1 onion, diced
3 celery sticks, finely sliced
1½ litre hot vegetable stock
Fresh coriander and
   crème fraîche to serve

1 Preheat the oven to 200°C/180°C Fan/400°F.
2 Melt 1 tablespoon of coconut oil with the spices and rosemary in a large roasting tin. Add the vegetables to the roasting tin and stir to evenly coat. Roast in the oven for 20 minutes.
3 Melt 2 teaspoons of coconut oil in a large saucepan over a low heat.
4 Add the garlic, onion and celery to the pan and lightly sauté until the onions are softened.
5 Add the roasted root vegetables to the pan and stir. Add the stock, bring to a boil, cover and return to a gentle simmer for 10 minutes.
6 Use a hand-held blender to blend the soup to your preferred consistency.
7 Serve with some freshly chopped coriander and crème fraîche.

Handy hint!

This recipe can be modified to a single root vegetable soup too – just increase the quantity of your chosen root vegetable to 500g.

MUSHROOM AND FENNEL SOUP

Mushroom soup is often very earthy and requires a lot of cream to lighten it up. Here I've used a blend of fennel and cashews to add creaminess and lightness. A little bit of white wine or Martini also helps!

Serves 4

2 fennel bulbs
1 tbsp coconut oil
2 cloves garlic, minced
2 medium onions, diced
500g mushrooms
   (button, chestnut or regular),
   peeled and quartered
1 litre hot vegetable stock
50ml white wine/Martini
50g cashew nuts
Freshly ground black pepper

1 For the fennel, remove the outer layer from the bulbs and chop off the feathery bit on top before cutting into cubes.

2 Melt the coconut oil over a medium heat in a large saucepan. Add the garlic and onions and gently cook until the onions are softened.

3 Add the chopped fennel and continue to cook for about 5 minutes.

4 Stir through the mushrooms while you prepare the stock.

5 Pour in the stock, white wine or Martini and cashew nuts. Bring the saucepan to a boil, cover and reduce to a simmer. Cook for 20–30 minutes until the mushrooms are soft through.

6 Add some freshly ground pepper and blend to your preferred consistency.

PEA, SPINACH AND SMOKED BACON SOUP

Bacon and cabbage is a weekly tradition in my family which means there's always some smoked bacon hiding in the fridge. This soup is a great way to use up leftover bacon, ham or rashers but will also work well without the bacon for a veggie option.

Serves 6

1 tsp coconut oil

1 onion, diced

2 cloves garlic, minced

200g leftover ham, smoked bacon or
   raw bacon lardons, diced

1 litre hot vegetable stock

300g spinach/kale, roughly torn

200g frozen peas

2 tbsp crème fraîche

1 Melt the coconut oil in a large saucepan over a medium heat. Add the onion and garlic and sauté until softened.

2 Add the bacon and continue to cook for a further 5 minutes while preparing the stock.

3 In a dry frying pan, gently wilt the spinach or kale before adding with the peas and vegetable stock to the saucepan. Bring to a boil, cover and reduce to a simmer for 20 minutes.

4 Blend to your desired consistency.

5 Stir through the crème fraîche before serving.

SPICED BUTTERNUT SQUASH SOUP

This was one of my first soup recipes on the blog and continues to be a firm favourite and regular lunchbox filler in work. Pumpkin or sweet potato are great substitutes for butternut squash when in season.

Serves 6

Coconut oil

2 tsp ground cumin

1 tsp ground turmeric

2 butternut squash, peeled and cubed

1 medium-sized onion, diced

3 cloves garlic, minced

1 litre hot vegetable stock

3 tbsp crème fraîche

For the herby nut topping:

2 tbsp dukkah (see page 85)

2 tbsp fresh parsley and coriander, roughly chopped

36ml extra-virgin olive oil

1 Preheat the oven to 200°C/180°C Fan/400°F.

2 Melt 1 tablespoon of coconut oil with the spices in a large roasting tray. Add the cubed butternut squash and mix through until well coated.

3 Roast in the oven for 30 minutes or until soft.

4 Melt 1 teaspoon of coconut oil in a large saucepan and sauté the onion and garlic while preparing the stock. Once the onion has softened, add in the roast squash and stock.

5 Bring to a boil, cover and reduce to a simmer for 10 minutes.

6 Stir in the crème fraîche and blend until smooth.

7 For the herby nut topping: stir all the ingredients together in a small bowl and swirl a generous teaspoonful over each bowl of soup to serve.

Handy hint!

Customise your soup by adding different toppings. I love to add fresh herbs, seeds, roast spiced chickpeas or shredded chicken.

SOUPS

CREAMY BROCCOLI AND CASHEW SOUP

A lot of shop-bought soup is heavily laden with both sugar and cream. I'm a firm believer in eating unprocessed food as you can control exactly what goes into your and your family's bodies. Cashews are a great way to add a depth of creamy flavour without any added dairy.

Serves 6

1 large head of broccoli
1 tsp coconut oil
2 celery sticks, finely sliced
1 medium onion, diced
2 cloves of garlic, minced
2 tsp ground cumin
1 tsp ground coriander
50g cashews
1 litre hot vegetable stock

1 Divide the broccoli into florets and finely chop the stalks.
2 Melt the coconut oil in a large saucepan over a medium heat.
3 Once melted, gently sauté the broccoli stalks, celery, onions and garlic.
4 When the onions and celery are softened, add the cumin and coriander and continue to cook for a further 2–3 minutes.
5 Add the stock, broccoli florets and cashews.
6 Bring to a boil, cover, reduce to a simmer and cook for about 20 minutes until the broccoli florets are soft through.
7 Blend the soup to a smooth texture and serve.

Variation

For a nut-free option, replace the cashews with 100ml crème fraiche or coconut milk.

ROAST TOMATO AND RED PEPPER SOUP

This soup is just gorgeous – it took me a while to achieve the flavour of a restaurant-style tomato soup but I got there in the end, so enjoy the results of my hard work!

As vine tomatoes can be expensive when out of season, use tinned whole tomatoes instead and roast them as described.

Serves 6

Coconut oil
2 sweet red peppers, destalked,
    deseeded and halved
500g ripe vine tomatoes or
    1 x 400g tinned whole tomatoes
1 large onion, diced
3 cloves of garlic, minced
3 tbsp fresh basil, roughly chopped
1 litre hot vegetable stock

1 Preheat the oven to 200°C/180°C Fan/400°F and melt 1 tablespoon of coconut oil in a large high-sided baking tray.
2 Once the oil is melted, add the red peppers and raw or tinned whole tomatoes. Roast for 30 minutes or until the skin blisters.
3 Sauté the onions and garlic over a medium heat until softened.
4 Stir through the roasted tomatoes, peppers, basil and stock.
5 Bring to the boil, cover, reduce to a simmer and cook for 5 minutes.
6 Blend until smooth using a hand-held blender.

BEETROOT AND CARROT SOUP

Earthiness, comfort and a little bit of spice are what this soup offers. I have a slight obsession with beetroot so it features in lots of my recipes!

Serves 6

2 tsp coconut oil

2 garlic cloves, minced

1 small red chilli, seeds removed
   and finely diced

1 red onion, diced

3 carrots, peeled and diced

2 celery sticks, finely sliced

6 medium raw beetroot, peeled and cubed

1 litre hot vegetable stock

2 large handfuls beetroot leaves
   and stalks/spinach/chard,
   roughly chopped

2 tbsp crème fraîche

1　Melt the coconut oil in a large saucepan over a low heat.

2　Add the garlic, chilli, onion, carrots and celery to the coconut oil and lightly sauté until the onions are softened.

3　Add the cubed beetroot and vegetable stock to the saucepan and bring to a boil.

4　Return to a gentle simmer, cover and cook for 20 minutes until the beetroot are tender.

5　Add the beetroot stalks and leaves to the soup.

6　Continue to cook for a further 5 minutes until the leaves have wilted and the stalks are tender.

7　Blend to your preferred texture. Serve with a dollop of crème fraîche or some crushed roasted hazelnuts.

Handy hint!

Wear gloves when handling the beetroot if you don't want to spend the rest of the day scrubbing your nails!

CREAMY ROAST CAULIFLOWER SOUP

Boiled cauliflower and roasted cauliflower are two completely different things. By roasting the cauliflower you get an almost nutty taste that is just wonderful as a side with dinner, but follow the recipe below to create a beautifully smooth and flavoursome soup.

Serves 4

Coconut oil

½ tsp salt

1 large cauliflower, divided into florets

5 cloves of garlic

2 sprigs of fresh rosemary or
   1 tsp dried mixed herbs

1 medium onion, diced

1 litre hot vegetable stock

1 tbsp crème fraîche

1 Preheat the oven to 200°C/180°C Fan/400°F and melt 1 tablespoon of the coconut oil in a large roasting tray.

2 Bring a large pot of water with the salt to the boil and reduce to a simmer.

3 Add the cauliflower florets and cook for 3–5 minutes until tender.

4 Remove with a slotted spoon and add to the roasting tray with the melted oil, unpeeled garlic and herbs.

5 Roast in the oven for 30–40 minutes or until soft through. Once cooked, save a few cauliflower florets to add as a garnish when serving. Squeeze the garlic from the skin and discard the skin.

6 Melt 1 teaspoon of coconut oil over a medium heat in a large saucepan, add the onion and sauté until softened.

7 Add the roasted cauliflower, peeled garlic and vegetable stock to the onion. Bring to the boil, cover, reduce to a simmer and cook for a further 5 minutes.

8 Stir through the crème fraîche and blend to your preferred consistency.

9 Serve with the reserved roasted cauliflower on top.

Super Salads

Eat the Rainbow Every Day

Cauliflower Tabbouleh   110

Charred Baby Gem   112

Potato Salad with Beetroot and Almond   112

Red Cabbage, Carrot and Seed Slaw   113

Mediterranean Quinoa and Bulgur Salad with Shredded Chicken   116

Tender-stem Broccoli, Spinach, Baby Gem and Vegetable Crisps   118

Beetroot, Freekeh, Cucumber and Mackerel   120

Broccoli, Feta, Tomato and Hazelnut   122

Carrot and Seed Slaw   122

Beetroot and Mozzarella Stacks   123

Kale, Roast Butternut Squash, Quinoa and Pomegranate   126

Crispy Asian Slaw with Cod and Roasted Cashews   128

Broccoli and Almond Turmeric Grains   130

Roast Vegetable and Cranberry Grains   132

SUPER SALADS

CAULIFLOWER TABBOULEH

Tabbouleh is a traditional Lebanese dish made with bulgur wheat or couscous. For this recipe, I've substituted cauliflower rice for grains, which is a great way to squeeze some extra vegetables into your day.

Serves 4

1 small head cauliflower (around 250g),
   leaves removed and cut into rough cubes
200ml vegetable stock
2 tbsp fresh lemon juice
1 tbsp sunflower seeds
1 tbsp pumpkin seeds
2 tbsp pistachios
2 tbsp each of fresh parsley,
   mint and coriander
4 tbsp pomegranate seeds

1 Blitz the cauliflower in a food processor until a rough rice consistency is formed.
2 Heat a large frying pan over a medium heat and add the cauliflower, stock and 1 tablespoon of lemon juice. Bring to the boil, cover with a lid and reduce to a simmer. Continue to cook until all the liquid is absorbed, stirring regularly to ensure the cauliflower cooks evenly and doesn't stick to the pan.
3 Transfer to a large mixing bowl and allow to cool.
4 Place all the seeds and pistachios in a dry frying pan. Toast over a medium heat until you hear the seeds pop.
5 Roughly chop all the fresh herbs and add to the cauliflower with the pomegranate seeds, toasted seeds and pistachios and remaining lemon juice.
6 Mix well together and serve.

Handy hint!

The cauliflower rice is also great served as a side with curries or stews instead of grain.

CHARRED BABY GEM

Let's be honest, lettuce is not the most exciting of vegetables. However, gently charring baby gem lettuce over a high heat and adding tahini and dukkah turns 'meh' into 'yeah' pretty quickly!

Serves 2

2 heads baby gem lettuce
1 tbsp extra-virgin olive oil
1 tbsp tahini
2 tsp dukkah (see page 85)

1 Remove the stalk tips of each lettuce head and cut lengthways in half. Roll each lettuce in olive oil.
2 Bring a dry grill pan to smoking point and reduce the heat a little before placing each lettuce onto the grill with a sizzle.
3 Flip over once nicely charred on one side.
4 Remove from the pan and sprinkle over the tahini and dukkah.

POTATO SALAD WITH BEETROOT AND ALMOND

I adore beetroot! The natural dye creates a vivid pink colour that I find really inviting and summery at any time of the year. New potatoes in season during the summer months are my favourite to use but baby potatoes available all year round are good substitutes.

Serves 4

2 tbsp crème fraîche
1 tbsp fresh lemon juice
300g baby potatoes, steamed,
   cooled and roughly cubed
2 cooked beetroot, roughly cubed
2 tbsp flaked almonds
1 tbsp fresh chives or parsley,
   finely chopped

1 In a mixing bowl, combine the crème fraîche and lemon juice.
2 Stir through the potatoes, beetroot and almonds until well coated.
3 Serve with a sprinkle of the chives or parsley.

RED CABBAGE, CARROT AND SEED SLAW

Red cabbage makes great coleslaw. Not only is it full of crunchy goodness but its colour gives your senses a real boost.

Serves 4

½ small red cabbage, thinly sliced
1 medium carrot, coarsely grated
2 spring onions, thinly sliced
2 tbsp pumpkin and sunflower seeds
3 tbsp Creamy Tahini Dressing
   (see page 87)

1 Place all the vegetables and seeds in a large mixing bowl.
2 Make the tahini dressing as per recipe until you get a smooth runny sauce.
3 Stir the dressing through the vegetables until well combined.

Handy hint!

If you find the dressing is too thick, just add more water and whisk again.

Charred Baby Gem, Potato Salad and Red Cabbage Slaw

MEDITERRANEAN QUINOA AND BULGUR SALAD WITH SHREDDED CHICKEN

This salad is sure to brighten up any lunchbox! The use of olives and sundried tomatoes instantly adds a real sense of the Mediterranean.

If you don't have bulgur wheat or quinoa in your cupboard then substitute with any blend of grains or lentils.

Serve with or without the chicken or another protein option.

Serves 4

1 tbsp extra-virgin olive oil

1 garlic clove, minced

1 tbsp fresh coriander, roughly chopped

1 tbsp fresh lemon juice

2 chicken fillets

90g bulgur wheat

110g quinoa, plain or multicoloured

235ml water

8 black olives, pitted and chopped

6 sundried tomatoes, chopped

50g feta cheese, cubed

2 tsp dried mixed herbs or fresh basil

2 tsp extra-virgin olive oil

1 For the shredded chicken: combine the oil, garlic, coriander and lemon together before pouring over the chicken in an ovenproof dish. Slowly roast in the oven at 140°C/120°C Fan/275°F for 25–30 minutes or until cooked through. Remove from the oven and allow to cool.

2 Whilst the chicken is cooking, place the bulgur wheat, quinoa and water in a saucepan and bring to a boil.

3 Cover, reduce to a simmer and continue to cook until all the water is absorbed.. Transfer to a large mixing bowl and allow to cool.

4 When the chicken is cooled, shred the chicken with two forks

5 Stir the olives, tomatoes, feta, herbs and oil through the cooked grains until well combined.

6 Divide amongst bowls and serve with the shredded chicken sprinkled on top.

TENDER-STEM BROCCOLI, SPINACH, BABY GEM AND VEGETABLE CRISPS

This salad is full of fresh, inviting flavours. The dressing combines hazelnuts and lemon to create a luxurious flavour. I love to serve this salad alongside my Citrus Chicken (see page 152) for a very quick and easy dinner.

Serves 4

2 tbsp hazelnuts

4 tbsp extra-virgin olive oil

1 tbsp lemon juice

Zest of ½ lemon

½ tsp salt

10 florets tender-stem or purple sprouting broccoli

1 head baby gem lettuce

2 large handfuls baby leaf spinach

1 large handful vegetable crisps

1   Place the hazelnuts in a dry frying pan over a medium heat and toast until the skin begins to loosen.

2   Save 1 tablespoon of the nuts for later, place the remaining hazelnuts in a food processor and blitz to a fine consistency or crush in a jar with a rolling pin.

3   Place the blitzed hazelnuts, oil, lemon juice and zest in a clean jar. Tighten the lid and shake to combine. Taste and add more lemon juice if you want a zestier flavour.

4   Bring a small pan of water with the salt to the boil, remove from the heat and add the broccoli. Blanch for 5 minutes, strain and rinse under running cold water until fully cool.

5   Halve the reserved toasted hazelnuts.

6   In a large mixing bowl, separate the leaves from the head of baby gem, add the spinach, broccoli, toasted halved hazelnuts and 2 tablespoons of the hazelnut and lemon oil. Mix it all together gently with your hands.

7   Transfer to a large serving platter and sprinkle the vegetable crisps over to finish.

Handy hint!

If short on time, the Frenchie dressing on page 86 also works well with this salad.

BEETROOT, FREEKEH, CUCUMBER AND MACKEREL

Freekeh is an ancient grain made from green durum wheat commonly used in Middle Eastern and North African cuisines. Durum wheat is known for its high protein content and low glycaemic index values so it's a great grain to keep you feeling fuller for longer.

Serves 4

90g freekeh grain

235ml water

2 large cooked beetroots, cubed

2 tbsp flaked almonds

¼ cucumber, cubed

1 celery stick, thinly sliced rounds

5 large fresh basil leaves, roughly chopped

2 fillets smoked mackerel

For the dressing:

2 tsp balsamic vinegar

1 tsp extra-virgin olive oil

1 tsp honey

2 tsp Dijon mustard

1 Rinse the freekeh in a sieve under a cold tap before adding with the water to a small saucepan. Bring to a boil, reduce to a simmer on the lowest heat, cover and continue to cook until all the water is absorbed. Remove from the heat, transfer to a mixing bowl and allow to cool.

2 Place the flaked almonds in a pan and gently toast over a low heat for a few minutes until they begin to brown.

3 Whisk together all the dressing ingredients until the mustard is well combined.

4 Add the beetroot, cucumber, celery and basil to the cooled freekeh.

5 Stir 4 teaspoons of the dressing through the freekeh mix.

6 Serve with the smoked mackerel and toasted almonds on top. Finish with another drizzle of dressing.

BROCCOLI, FETA, TOMATO AND HAZELNUT

Gently toasting the hazelnuts adds a great burst of flavour to complement the feta cheese.

Serves 4

2 tbsp hazelnuts
½ head of broccoli, divided into florets
½ tsp salt
8 cherry tomatoes, halved
50g feta cheese, cubed
3 tbsp Frenchie dressing
   (see page 86)

1 Place the hazelnuts in a dry frying pan over a medium heat and gently toast until the skin begins to loosen. Remove from the pan and allow to cool before cutting in half.
2 Place the broccoli florets in a bowl with the salt and cover with boiling water. After 5 minutes, strain and cool under a running cold tap until the broccoli is fully cooled.
3 Place the broccoli, hazelnuts and all the remaining ingredients in a bowl. Stir through the dressing until well combined.

CARROT AND SEED SLAW

This is a simple salad bursting with great colour, texture and flavours.

Serves 4

2 carrots, coarsely grated
1 tbsp sesame seeds
1 tbsp poppy seeds
1 tbsp pumpkin seeds
1 tbsp sunflower seeds
2 tbsp Frenchie dressing
   (see page 86)

1 Place all the ingredients in a large mixing bowl and combine together.

BEETROOT AND MOZZARELLA STACKS

These look really impressive but are so easy to make. They work great as a simple starter too.

Makes 4

1 tbsp hazelnuts
2 pre-cooked beetroot,
 sliced into rounds
2 fresh mozzarella balls,
 strained and sliced
2 tsp honey

1 Place the hazelnuts in a dry frying pan over a medium heat and gently toast until the skin begins to loosen. Allow the hazelnuts to cool before crushing into a coarse mixture. Either using a food processor or place in a jar and crush with the bottom of a rolling pin.
2 Create layered stacks with the beetroot and mozzarella slices.
3 Finish with a drizzle of honey and a teaspoon of crushed hazelnuts.

Variations

• Replace the mozzarella with soft goat's cheese or cottage cheese.
• Roast butternut squash slices are a delicious alternative to beetroot.

Broccoli and Tomato, Carrot Slaw and Beetroot Stacks

KALE, ROAST BUTTERNUT SQUASH, QUINOA AND POMEGRANATE

Roasting is such an easy way to make vegetables instantly more flavoursome. There are often vegetables lurking in the bottom of the fridge that look a little past their best. Once you peel them and remove any bad bits, they are ready for roasting.

This salad also works great with pumpkin, sweet potato, carrot or parsnip instead of butternut squash.

Serves 4

2 tsp coconut oil
300g butternut squash, peeled and cubed
½ tsp ground cumin
½ tsp ground turmeric
90g quinoa
235ml water
2 large handfuls kale, destalked
   and roughly torn
½ tsp sea salt
3 tbsp pomegranate seeds
2 tbsp fresh coriander, roughly chopped
2 tbsp fresh lemon juice
1 tbsp extra-virgin olive oil

1 Preheat the oven to 200°C/180°C Fan/400°F and melt the coconut oil in a large roasting tray.
2 Mix the butternut squash with the spices and coconut oil on the tray and roast in the oven for 20 minutes or until soft through.
3 Remove from the oven and allow to cool.
4 Bring the quinoa and water to the boil, reduce to the lowest heat, cover and continue to cook until all the water is absorbed. Remove from heat and allow to cool.
5 In a large mixing bowl, roughly tear the kale and massage in the salt until the kale turns dark green in colour.
6 Add the quinoa, squash, pomegranate, coriander, lemon juice and oil and mix together well.

CRISPY ASIAN SLAW WITH COD AND ROASTED CASHEWS

This salad is just bursting with fresh and crisp flavours. I love to travel, and this salad is inspired by traditional Thai and Vietnamese dishes that I have sampled. These cuisines have a strong focus on using the freshest ingredients in a simple way to showcase the flavours.

Serves 4

2 cod fillets
1 tsp coconut oil
50g cashew nuts
2 garlic cloves, peeled, thinly sliced
120g king prawns, pre-cooked

For the dressing:
3 large fresh coriander stalks without
    leaves, finely chopped
Sea salt
1 clove garlic, minced
1 fresh green chilli, de-seeded
    and finely chopped
1 tbsp sugar
1 tbsp fish sauce
1 tbsp water

For the salad:
2 heads bok choy, thinly sliced
4 radish, thinly sliced in rounds
1/3 cucumber, halved, cored
    and thinly sliced
1 shallot, diced
2 tbsp fresh coriander,
    roughly chopped
2 tbsp fresh mint leaves,
    roughly chopped

1 Bake the cod fillets whole in an ovenproof dish at 180°C/160°C Fan/350°F for 30 minutes.

2 Melt the coconut oil in a small baking tray and add the cashews and sliced garlic. Stir until well coated in oil and roast for 8 minutes or until crispy. Remove from the oven and allow to cool.

3 For the dressing: place the chopped coriander stalk in a pestle and mortar or a mug, mix through a pinch of sea salt and pound with a mortar or the bottom of a rolling pin until fragrant.

4 Add the minced garlic, finely chopped chilli, sugar, fish sauce and water. Stir to combine. Taste and you should get an equal balance of heat, salt, sour and sweet.

5 If one flavour overpowers the other; simply add more of the missing flavour to your taste.

6 Place all the vegetables in a large mixing bowl and add the dressing, prawns and roasted garlic and cashews (save some for a garnish) to the salad. Flake through the baked cod and combine well together.

7 Serve in heaped bowls with the remaining cashews and garlic on top.

THE GRAIN DUO

Whole grains are a necessary part of all our diets. Two of my favourites are bulgur wheat and quinoa. They are easy to cook, will keep well in the fridge and can be added to any kind of salad or served with a main dish. They are also super to mop up the juices from a curry.

Both of these salads can be made at the start of the week, or just cook the grains, then mix and match vegetable ingredients as the week goes on for lunch or dinner.

Both salads serve 4

BROCCOLI AND ALMOND TURMERIC GRAINS

45g bulgur wheat

45g quinoa

230ml water

1 tsp ground turmeric

½ broccoli, cut into florets

Pinch of salt

12 mangetout, thinly sliced

2 large fistfuls spinach

1 x 400g tin kidney beans,
   drained and rinsed

2 tbsp almonds

1 tbsp fresh lemon juice

2 tbsp extra-virgin olive oil

1 tsp apple cider vinegar

1 Place the grains, water and turmeric in a saucepan. Bring to a boil, reduce the heat to a simmer, cover and continue to cook for 5 minutes. Remove from the heat, transfer to a large mixing bowl and fluff up the grains with a fork.

2 Place the broccoli in a heatproof bowl sprinkle over the salt and cover with boiling water. Allow to blanch for 5 minutes or until just tender.

3 Strain and refresh under running cold water until fully cooled.

4 Place the cooked grains, blanched broccoli and all other remaining ingredients in a large mixing bowl and stir together.

5 Serve on a large plate or store in an airtight container in the fridge.

SUPER SALADS

ROAST VEGETABLE AND CRANBERRY GRAINS

1 tbsp coconut oil

1 small cauliflower, cut into florets

1 medium carrot, cut into batons

45g bulgur wheat

45g quinoa

230ml water

2 tbsp dried cranberries

1 tbsp garam masala (or ½ tsp ground
   cinnamon, 2 tsp ground cumin and
   ½ tsp ground coriander)

2 tbsp fresh parsley, roughly chopped

2 tbsp extra-virgin olive oil

Zest of ½ lemon

1 tbsp fresh lemon juice

1 Preheat the oven to 200°C/180°C Fan/400°F.

2 Melt the coconut oil in a large roasting tray. Once melted, stir through the cauliflower and carrot and roast in the oven for 20 minutes.

3 Place the grains and water in a saucepan. Bring to a boil, reduce the heat to a simmer, cover and continue to cook for 5 minutes. Remove from the heat, transfer to a large mixing bowl and fluff up the grains with a fork.

4 Whilst the grains and vegetables cook, place the dried cranberries in a small bowl and cover with boiling water to rehydrate.

5 Add the roasted vegetables and all other remaining ingredients to the cooked grains.

6 Strain the cranberries and stir through.

7 Serve on a large plate or store in an airtight container in the fridge.

The Main Affair

Some for Now and Later

Chicken and Beans 136

Courgetti Prawn 138

Baked Cod with Nettle Pesto and Cherry Tomatoes 140

Chicken and Grain Traybake 142

Ginger, Chicken and Chickpea Curry 144

Burrito Beef Bowl with Mexican Bean Salsa 146

Creamy Fish Pie 148

Sticky Sesame Pork and Greens 150

Citrus Chicken with Broccoli Rice 152

Grilled Salmon with Pesto and Roasted Stuffed Sweet Potato 154

Beef Steak with Salsa Verde and Rainbow Chips 156

Millet, Butternut Squash and Linseed Burgers 158

Bulgur Wheat, Quinoa and Beetroot Risotto 160

Beetroot, Feta and Black Bean Burgers 162

Vietnamese Filled Coconut Crepes 164

Goat's Cheese, Black Olive, Tomato and Courgette Tart 166

Red Pepper, Spinach and Brie Frittata 168

Creamy Apricot and Almond Turkey 170

Crispy Fish Tacos 172

Squash Noodles with Garlic Prawns 174

CHICKEN AND BEANS

Some of my friends decided to challenge me to create a recipe using chicken and beans and this was the result.

Serve this dish with rice, mashed potatoes, root vegetables or steamed green vegetables. For a vegetarian option, replace the chicken and bacon with large chunks of pumpkin, squash or potato.

Serves 5

2 tsp coconut oil

500g ripe vine tomatoes
  or 1 x 400g tinned whole tomatoes

2 sweet red peppers,
  de-seeded and halved

3 rashers or 50g bacon lardons,
  chopped

1 medium onion, finely chopped

2 cloves garlic, minced

1 tsp dried mixed herbs

½ tsp ground cumin

½ tsp paprika

1 tbsp Tabasco or hot chilli sauce

1 tbsp balsamic vinegar

1 x 400g tin cannellini or
  butter beans, drained and rinsed

1 x 400g tin kidney beans,
  drained and rinsed

3 large handfuls spinach

5 chicken breasts/thighs

1 Preheat the oven to 180°C/160°C Fan/350°F.

2 Melt one teaspoon of coconut oil in a large roasting tray and add the tomatoes and peppers. Roast in the oven for 25–30 minutes or until the skin blisters.

3 Over a medium heat, fry the chopped rashers in a large saucepan. Once nicely browned, remove to the side and rinse the pan.

4 Melt the remaining coconut oil over a medium heat in the clean saucepan. Sauté the onion and garlic until softened.

5 Add the cooked rashers, dried herbs, spices, chilli sauce, balsamic vinegar and roasted tomatoes and peppers to the pan. Continue to cook until the sauce begins to bubble.

6 Remove from the heat and blitz until smooth with a hand stick blender. (At this stage you could place the sauce into a container, cool fully before placing in the fridge or freezer for future use.)

7 Return the sauce to a low heat and stir through the beans and spinach before transferring to a large ovenproof dish.

8 Rinse the saucepan and brown the chicken on all sides.

9 Nestle the chicken amongst the bean mix and cook in the oven for 20–25 minutes until the chicken is cooked through.

Handy hints!

- The tomato based sauce can be prepared ahead and frozen in batches or stored in the fridge.
- The sauce works great as a base for pasta dishes or mixed through some mince, shredded chicken or vegetables for a quick and easy dinner.

COURGETTI PRAWN

Little did I think when I posted this on the blog that it would become the most viewed recipe! I can see why, as it's the perfect light treat for a made-in-minutes midweek dinner.

Who doesn't love a creamy pasta dish? I've substituted the pasta with courgetti (courgette spaghetti) and the cream with crème fraîche for a lighter option.

If you are not a fish lover, use chicken or pork. Make it veggie by adding chunks of steamed or roasted butternut squash.

Serves 2

75g frozen peas
1 courgette
50g butter
2 generous tbsp crème fraîche
1 tbsp fresh lemon juice
1 tbsp parmesan, finely grated
100g smoked salmon, roughly sliced
100g defrosted cooked prawns

1. Defrost the peas in a bowl of lukewarm water.
2. Use a julienne peeler or spiraliser (if you have neither, thinly slice the courgette into long slices) to create spaghetti-like courgette strips.
3. Bring a pan of salted water to the boil, remove from the heat and blanch the courgetti for 5 minutes. Strain and rinse until running cold water until fully cooled.
4. Melt the butter in a large saucepan over a low heat, stir in the crème fraîche, lemon juice and grated parmesan until well combined.
5. Stir through the smoked salmon, prawns, peas and strained courgetti until well combined and fully warm.
6. Serve in deep bowls with another sprinkle of parmesan on top and a squeeze of lemon juice.

BAKED COD WITH NETTLE PESTO AND CHERRY TOMATOES

This recipe is very special to me as I entered it in a competition and ended up representing Ireland in Paris at the 2015 Cono Sur Food Bloggers final. The recipe takes only minutes to assemble and the oven will do the rest.

I make my own nettle pesto from wild nettles foraged from the fields around my house. Any pesto works great, though. See page 82 for a selection of my favourites.

Serves 2

1 large sweet potato

2 cod fillets

10 cherry tomatoes, halved

4 tsp nettle pesto (see page 84)

1 tbsp butter

1 Preheat the oven to 180°C/160°C Fan/350°F.

2 Place the sweet potato whole in the oven and bake until soft through.

3 Line a baking tray or oven-proof dish with tin-foil or parchment.

4 Pat the fish dry on a paper towel before placing skin side down onto the foil. Spoon over the pesto to evenly cover the fish.

5 Layer the tomato slices on top and place in the oven for 20 minutes.

6 Scoop the baked sweet potato out from the skin and mash with the butter until smooth.

7 Serve the cod on a bed of mashed sweet potatoes.

CHICKEN AND GRAIN TRAYBAKE

Dinner doesn't get much easier than a traybake. Simply arrange the grains, meat and vegetables, pour over the marinade and pop in the oven.

Replace the fennel with leeks, peppers or whatever vegetables you have at hand. As always, switch the grains to suit your cupboard stock too.

Serves 4

190g bulgur wheat
190g freekeh grain
1 fennel bulb
Coconut oil
4 chicken thighs/legs/breasts
3 carrots, cut into batons
2 celery sticks, cut into batons

For the marinade:
5 cloves garlic, minced
1 inch fresh ginger, grated
1 tsp ground cumin
½ tsp ground coriander
1 tsp honey
2 tbsp balsamic vinegar
1 tbsp apple cider vinegar
1 tbsp extra-virgin olive oil
300ml hot water

1. Preheat the oven to 180°C/160°C Fan/350°F.
2. Place the freekeh and bulgur wheat in a bowl and cover with water.
3. Peel the fennel, cut off the feathery top and hard centre, cut in half lengthways.
4. Place 1 teaspoon coconut oil in a frying pan, add the chicken and brown on all sides.
5. Strain and rinse the soaked freekeh and bulgur wheat. Place in the bottom of a large ovenproof or casserole dish. Arrange the vegetables and browned chicken on top.
6. Mix together the garlic, ginger, spices, honey, vinegars and oil in a small bowl until well combined.
7. Pour the marinade over the dish and add the hot water.
8. Bake in the oven for 45–50 minutes until all the liquid is absorbed.

GINGER, CHICKEN AND CHICKPEA CURRY

This is my favourite dinner. I just love coming home from work and tucking into a big bowl of this curry. The spices naturally warm you from the inside out – perfect for a cold day.

Curries are great for feeding friends, freezer dinners and as simple lunchbox fillers. Swap sweet potato, butternut squash or parsnip in place of the turnip as you wish. Any fruit chutney will combine well with the curry instead of the relish. I tend to serve this curry on a bed of quinoa, bulgur wheat or steamed green vegetables.

For vegetarian friends, just omit the chicken and increase the vegetables.

Serves 8

Coconut oil
2 onions, finely diced
3 cloves garlic, minced
2 inch length of fresh ginger, grated
1 medium turnip, bite-sized chunks
3 large carrots, semi-circle slices
1 tbsp ground turmeric
2 heaped tbsp curry powder
1 x 400g tin coconut milk
1 x 400g tin chopped tomatoes
4 tsp vegetable stock
5 chicken fillets, chunky cubes
1 x 400g tin chickpeas, drained and rinsed
2 tbsp tomato relish

1   Heat 2 teaspoons of coconut oil in a large saucepan over a medium heat. Add the onion, garlic and ginger and gently sauté until softened.
2   Add the turnip and carrots to the pan and stir through the spices.
3   Pour in the coconut milk, chopped tomatoes and vegetable stock. Bring to a gentle simmer with the lid on for 20–30 minutes until the turnip is soft through.
4   Brown the chicken in a frying pan over a medium heat, season with some pepper and add to the vegetable mix.
5   Stir through the chickpeas and relish to the saucepan. Gently simmer for 10 minutes with the lid off to cook the chicken through.
6   Serve as you like.

BURRITO BEEF BOWL WITH MEXICAN BEAN SALSA

A burrito bowl is the perfect last-minute dinner. This bean salsa is great to have at any time of year to provide your senses with a boost of colour and flavour.

For a veggie option, replace the beef with diced carrots, courgette or cooked green or brown lentils.

Serve with some fresh salad leaves, on a bed of steamed greens, spoon into toasted pittas or add sweet potato wedges on the side.

Serves 4

Coconut oil
8 spring onions, finely sliced
4 cloves garlic, minced
4 celery sticks, finely sliced
80g mushrooms, finely sliced
10 cherry tomatoes, quartered
500g steak mince
2 tsp paprika
2 tsp ground cumin
40g dark chocolate, chopped
   into chunks

1 Melt 2 teaspoons coconut oil in a frying pan over a low heat. Sauté the spring onions, garlic, celery and mushrooms for 5 minutes until the mushrooms are cooked through. Add the tomatoes and continue to cook for another 2 minutes. Remove from the pan and set aside.

2 Return the frying pan to the heat and brown the mince with the spices before adding back in the vegetables.

3 Stir through the chocolate until melted.

4 Add 1–2 tablespoons of water to the mix if you find it a little dry.

MEXICAN BEAN SALSA

2 fresh corn on the cob or
   1 x 400g tin corn, drained
1 x 400g tin kidney beans,
   drained and rinsed
8 cherry tomatoes, quartered
2 spring onions, finely sliced
1 fistful fresh coriander,
   roughly chopped
Juice of ½ fresh lime

1 If using fresh corn, cook the corn on the cob in a pan of boiling water for 20 minutes or until tender. Once cooked, heat a grill pan until smoking point and lightly char the corn on all sides.

2 Allow to cool and cut the corn off the cob with a long knife.

3 Place all the vegetables and beans in a large bowl, mix through the coriander and lime juice.

SPICY SWEET POTATO WEDGES

4 tsp coconut oil, melted

2 tsp paprika

2 large sweet potato, cut into wedges

1   Preheat the oven to 200°C/180°C fan/400°F. In a roasting tray, mix the coconut oil and paprika together before stirring through the sweet potato wedges until well coated.

2   Roast in the oven for 25–30 minutes or until soft through.

Speed things up by pre-cooking the potatoes whole for a few minutes on high in the microwave before cutting, mixing with the oil and paprika and baking in the oven for a crispy finish.

CREAMY FISH PIE

Fish is an easy and quick source of protein and essential fatty acids. Any combination of white and smoked fish can be used in this pie. Add shredded spinach, kale or broccoli to boost your vegetable intake. I prefer to serve the pie with steamed vegetables or a mixed salad.

Serves 6

2 medium-sized sweet potatoes, peeled and cut into chunks
5 tbsp frozen peas
500g smoked fish (haddock/coley)
500g white fish (cod/hake/pollock)
5 tbsp milk
1 tsp coconut oil
2 large leeks, thinly sliced
10 button mushrooms, thinly sliced
100g smoked salmon, roughly sliced
3 tbsp crème fraîche
1 tbsp fresh lemon juice
Freshly ground pepper

1 Preheat the oven to 200°C/180°C Fan/400°F.
2 Steam the sweet potato until soft through.
3 Cover the frozen peas in a bowl with lukewarm water to defrost.
4 Place all the fresh fish into a large oven-proof dish and add the milk. Cover with a lid or parchment and place in the pre-heated oven for 10 minutes or until the fish begins to flake. Remove and set aside.
5 Gently melt the coconut oil in a large saucepan, add the leeks and mushrooms and gently sauté until soft. Drain the peas and add with the smoked salmon to the leeks and mushrooms
6 Flake the fish into the pan, discarding any skin or bones and mix well.
7 Stir in the crème fraîche and lemon juice.
8 Once well combined return mix to ovenproof dish. Mash the sweet potato with some pepper and layer over the fish mix.
9 Place in the oven for 35 minutes or until the dish is bubbling nicely.

Variation

Replace the sweet potato with any mashed root vegetable or regular potatoes.

STICKY SESAME PORK AND GREENS

The freshest green beans you can get your hands on work best with this recipe to ensure a crunchy texture in contrast to the pork. Toasted sesame oil is a great item to have in your kitchen cupboard as it really livens up any salad or stir-fry.

Serves 4

180g green beans, topped and tailed
1 pork steak, thinly sliced
Coconut oil
1 red onion, thinly sliced
2 spring onions, thinly sliced
3 tbsp sesame seeds
4 tbsp soy or tamari sauce
2 tbsp toasted sesame oil
3 tbsp water
2 tbsp apple cider vinegar

1 Bring a small saucepan of salted water to the boil, remove from the heat and add the green beans for 5 minutes with the lid on.
2 Drain and refresh the beans under running cold water until cool. Leave to one side. The beans should be cooked but still have a bite.
3 Place a large frying pan over a high heat and add the sliced pork steak (you should hear a sizzle as the meat hits the pan).
4 Brown the meat on all sides before removing from the pan.
5 Reduce the pan to a medium heat, add 1 teaspoon of coconut oil to the pan and sauté the red onion. Once cooked through, add the green beans, spring onions, sesame seeds and cooked pork.
6 Add the remaining ingredients; increase the heat to high and cook through for a further 3–5 minutes, gently stirring together.
7 Serve with brown rice or a grain of your choice.

Variation

For a veggie option, replace the pork with sliced aubergine or butternut squash.

CITRUS CHICKEN WITH BROCCOLI RICE

This is a great midweek dish as, with a little bit of preparation the night before, you'll have your dinner on the table in minutes. Marinate the chicken the night before and leave in the fridge, whilst the broccoli can be blitzed raw and stored in the fridge too.

Serves 4

For the marinade:

4 cloves garlic, minced

1 inch sized piece of fresh ginger, grated

Juice of 1 orange

Juice of ½ lemon

1 tbsp extra-virgin olive oil

4 tbsp water

1 tbsp mixed herbs

1 tsp freshly ground pepper

4 chicken fillets

1 large broccoli

30ml water

3 large handfuls of kale, de-stalked and roughly chopped

6 spring onions, finely sliced

4 tbsp crème fraîche

1. For the marinade: stir together all the ingredients in a large bowl.
2. Cut the chicken breasts into generous strips and add to the marinade. Cover and place in the fridge for at least 40 minutes or overnight.
3. For the broccoli rice: chop the broccoli including the stalk into florets and coarsely blitz with a food processor.
4. Place the broccoli rice with the water in a frying pan over a medium heat. Once the water begins to bubble, cover with a lid and allow the broccoli to gently steam for 5 minutes.
5. Reduce the heat to low and stir through the kale, spring onions and crème fraîche. Cover with the lid and allow the kale and scallions to lightly cook.
6. Preheat a grill pan over a high heat.
7. Add the chicken to the pan, keeping some marinade aside.
8. Cook the chicken through, reduce the heat, spoon over the remaining marinade and cook for a further 2–3 minutes.
9. Serve the chicken on top of a bed of broccoli rice.

THE MAIN AFFAIR

GRILLED SALMON WITH PESTO AND ROASTED STUFFED SWEET POTATO

This is one of my favourite dinners to have the night before a big match. I love how light the salmon is while combining with the slow-release carbohydrates of sweet potato alongside a green salad.

Serves 2

1 large sweet potato

2 salmon darnes

2 handfuls kale, de-stalked and roughly chopped

½ tsp sea salt

¼ cucumber, halved, cored, thinly sliced

2 celery sticks, thinly sliced

2 tbsp cottage cheese

2 tsp coriander pesto (see page 83)

1 Bake the sweet potato whole in the oven at 200°C/180°C Fan/400°F for 30 minutes or in a microwave on high for 5 minutes until soft through.

2 Place a grill pan over a medium heat until it begins to smoke. Place the salmon skin side down and grill until crisp. Flip over and cook on the opposite side.

3 In a bowl, roughly tear the kale and massage through the salt. Add the cucumber and celery.

4 Divide the vegetables amongst the two plates. Halve the sweet potato, place 1 tablespoon of cottage cheese on each and drizzle the pesto over the salmon

Handy hint!

Remove the core from the cucumber by first halving it lengthways. Then use a spoon to scoop out the seeds whilst keeping the shape intact.

BEEF STEAK WITH SALSA VERDE AND RAINBOW CHIPS

I love my vegetables but I also love meat and I think you can't beat a good steak! The quality of meat is so important to the taste, no matter how good or bad a cook you are. Go visit your local butcher to find the best quality and locally sourced beef available to you.

Serves 2

2 carrots, peeled

2 parsnips, peeled

2 tbsp extra-virgin olive oil

2 sirloin steaks

Sea salt

For the salsa verde:

20g fresh coriander
  (include the stalks)

20g fresh parsley

20g fresh mint leaves

½ red onion, finely diced

2 tbsp fresh lemon juice

Zest of ½ a lemon

1 tbsp rapeseed oil

3 tbsp extra-virgin olive oil

1 Preheat the oven to 200°C/180°C Fan/400°F.

2 Slice the vegetables into thin chips. Mix 1 tablespoon of the oil through the vegetables, scatter over a roasting tray and roast in the oven for 25 minutes or until beginning to crisp.

3 Remove the steak from the fridge and massage some fresh sea salt into the meat before massaging through the remaining olive oil. Leave the meat out at room temperature until ready to cook.

4 Prepare the salsa verde: bunch all the herbs together into a ball and roughly chop.

5 Place in a bowl and mix together with the red onion, lemon juice, zest and oils.

6 Bring a grill pan to smoking point over a high heat before adding the steak (you should hear a sizzle as the meat hits the pan) and cook to your preferred taste. Allow the meat to rest off the heat for at least five minutes before serving.

7 Serve with the roasted vegetable chips and the salsa verde.

Handy hints!

- I know it might be tempting to prod and poke at the meat when it's on the pan but try not to as you are removing the heat from the meat. The secret is to make sure the pan is really hot before adding the meat, so if you don't hear a sizzle, simply remove the meat and wait a bit longer.
- Celeriac or beetroot are great additions to the rainbow chips.

Variation

Serve with a Creamy Garlic Mushroom Sauce

1 tsp coconut oil, 2 minced cloves garlic, 60g thinly sliced mushrooms, 25g butter, 50g crème fraîche, 2 tsp dried mixed herbs

1. Melt the coconut oil in a small frying pan over a medium heat.
2. Add the garlic and mushrooms and cook until beginning to brown. Set aside from the pan.
3. Melt the butter and crème fraîche together, add the herbs and bring to a gentle simmer until the sauce begins to thicken. Return the mushrooms and garlic to the pan and stir through.
4. Remove from heat and reheat before serving over the steak.

THE MAIN AFFAIR

MILLET, BUTTERNUT SQUASH AND LINSEED BURGERS

These burgers were inspired by the wonderful cooking of Kai Café in Galway city. The ingredient combination of the burgers really interested me so I naturally had to taste them. I loved them so much that I attempted to recreate them in my own kitchen; I hope I captured the magical taste.

Instead of millet grain you could use quinoa, bulgur wheat or rice. You can also replace the cashew nut butter with any nut butter you have in stock at home or exclude completely from the sauce.

Makes 12 burgers

Coconut oil
1 whole butternut squash,
    halved and de-seeded
200g millet grain
450mls water
½ tsp salt
1 red onion, thinly sliced
3 cloves garlic, minced
1 tsp ground coriander
¾ tsp ground cumin
¾ tsp ground turmeric
½ tsp paprika
½ tsp ground ginger
3 tbsp plain yoghurt
1 egg, beaten
3 tbsp fresh coriander, chopped
3 tbsp brown linseed

1   Preheat the oven to 220°C/200°C Fan/425°F. Melt 2 teaspoons of coconut oil in a large roasting tin.

2   Use a sharp knife to cross-hatch the inside of the butternut squash flesh. Place the squash skin side up on the roasting tin. Roast in the oven for 40 minutes until the skin blisters and the flesh is soft through.

3   Place the millet, water and salt in a saucepan. Bring to a boil, cover, reduce to a simmer and continue to cook for at least 15–20 minutes or until all the water is absorbed. Transfer to a large mixing bowl and allow to cool.

4   Melt 1 teaspoon of coconut oil in a large frying pan over a medium heat. Sauté the red onion and garlic together until soft through. Reduce the heat and stir through the spices until fragrant. Remove and add to the cooled millet.

5   Remove the butternut squash from the oven and spoon out the cooked flesh. Reduce the oven heat to 200°C/180°C Fan/400°F.

6   Add the cooked squash, yoghurt, egg, coriander and linseed to the millet and combine well together.

7   Line two baking trays with parchment.

For the cashew sauce:

1 tbsp cashew nut butter

2 tbsp apple cider vinegar

1 tbsp extra-virgin olive oil

2 tsp tahini

1 tbsp plain yoghurt

2 tbsp water

½ tsp ground cumin

8 Using damp hands shape 1 tablespoon of the mixture at a time into burgers and place onto the trays. Repeat with remaining mixture.

9 Bake in the oven for 25–30 minutes or until firm on the outside.

10 For the cashew sauce: whisk all the ingredients together in a bowl until well combined. If you like sauces a little bit more runny just add more water until you achieve your preferred consistency.

11 Serve warm with a drizzle of the cashew sauce alongside a green salad.

THE MAIN AFFAIR

BULGUR WHEAT, QUINOA AND BEETROOT RISOTTO

I love this dish on a cold autumn or winter's night. It works great served with some flaked smoked mackerel on top or alongside some wilted greens like kale, spinach or courgette.

Beetroot packs a serious colour punch that's sure to brighten up any day and I can't get enough of it.

Serves 5

1 tsp coconut oil
3 cloves garlic, minced
1 large onion, diced
2 celery sticks, thinly sliced
80g mushrooms, thinly sliced
1 tbsp dried mixed herbs
100g quinoa
100g bulgur wheat
250ml white wine
750ml hot vegetable stock
200g pre-cooked or raw beetroot, cubed
2 tbsp crème fraîche
Parmesan

1. Melt the coconut oil in a large saucepan over a medium heat.
2. Add the garlic, onions and celery and lightly sauté until the onions are softened.
3. Add the mushrooms and continue to cook until soft.
4. Stir through the dried herbs, quinoa and bulgur wheat until well combined. Add the white wine to de-glaze the pan.
5. Add a ladle of hot stock to the pan, stir to combine until absorbed. Continue to stir through each ladle of stock until well absorbed. Cover the pan with a lid and allow to cook for 10–15 minutes until the grain is tender.
6. Reduce the heat to a simmer, add the beetroot and stir through the mix with the crème fraîche. Allow to cook for a further 5 minutes if using pre-cooked beetroot or 15 minutes if using fresh beetroot until you get a bright and vibrant colour from the beetroot.
7. Serve the risotto topped with freshly grated parmesan.

Handy hint!

To freeze: simply divide amongst containers and allow to cool fully before placing in the freezer.

BEETROOT, FETA AND BLACK BEAN BURGERS

I adore these as a quick dinner in the evening after a long day. I usually make a big batch of these burgers and freeze them in pairs. All I have to do is defrost the burgers in the microwave whilst I prepare a salad to serve alongside them and dinner is served.

Makes 8 medium-sized burgers

140g walnuts
500g cooked beetroot,
    coarsely grated
100g feta, cubed
6 spring onions, finely sliced
1 fistful fresh/frozen mint leaves,
    roughly chopped
1 tbsp fresh lemon juice
1 x 400g tin black beans,
    drained and rinsed

To serve:
Burger buns or pittas
Salad leaves
Crème fraîche
Avocado
Tomato relish

1 Preheat the oven to 180°C/160°C Fan/350°F.

2 Place the walnuts in a roasting tray and roast for 8 minutes until they begin to crisp. Remove from the oven and roughly chop.

3 In a large mixing bowl place the beetroot, feta, spring onions, mint leaves, lemon juice and chopped walnuts.

4 Gently mash or pulse the black beans with a hand-held blender or food processor.

5 Add the black beans to the other ingredients and gently mix together until well combined.

6 Increase the oven temperature to 200°C/180°C Fan/400°F and line two baking trays with parchment.

7 Using damp hands, shape 1 tablespoon of the beetroot mix at a time into burgers of whatever size you like. Repeat with remaining mixture.

8 Add each burger to the baking trays and gently press down with the back of a spoon.

9 Bake in the oven for 30 minutes, gently turning the burgers half way through.

10 Serve in a toasted burger bun or pitta with some relish, salad leaves, crème fraîche and avocado.

VIETNAMESE FILLED COCONUT CREPES

These crepes are light and fluffy. The filling is based on Banh Xeo – a traditional Vietnamese dish I experienced whilst backpacking around the country with friends. If you ever get the chance, go and visit Vietnam and experience the amazing food markets, restaurants and some of the freshest ingredients imaginable.

Serves 2, makes 2 crepes

For the crepes:

2 eggs

80ml tinned coconut milk

½ tsp ground turmeric

Coconut oil

2 tbsp coconut flour
  (or 60g plain white/rice flour)

For the filling:

1 pork chop, thinly sliced

150g pre-cooked frozen prawns, defrosted

2 garlic cloves, minced

1 tbsp fish sauce

½ tsp sugar

2 tbsp sesame oil

½ onion, thinly sliced

6 chestnut mushrooms, thinly sliced

2 spring onions, thinly sliced

100g beansprouts

2 tbsp frozen green peas, defrosted

1 tablespoon fresh mint and coriander,
  roughly chopped

1 For the crepe batter: in a measuring jug whisk together the eggs, coconut milk, turmeric and 2 tablespoons of melted coconut oil. Add the coconut flour and whisk again until well combined.

2 For the filling: combine the pork, prawns, garlic, fish sauce, sugar and sesame oil in a large bowl.

3 Heat 1 teaspoon of coconut oil in a large frying pan over a medium heat and fry the sliced onion until softened. Add the pork and prawn mixture and continue to cook until the pork is cooked through. Remove and set aside.

4 To make the crepes: heat 1 teaspoon of coconut oil in a non-stick frying pan over a medium heat. Add half the batter and cook for a minute on one side until it begins to bubble.

5 To half of the crepe, add half of the pork and prawn mix followed by some mushrooms, spring onions, beansprouts and peas. Fold over the other half and continue to cook until the mushroom softens. Remove from the pan and repeat with the remaining batter and filling.

6 Serve with some fresh mint and coriander.

Handy hint!

Prepare the crepe batter and filling ahead and store in the fridge. Simply whisk the batter again before using to ensure no lumps.

GOAT'S CHEESE, BLACK OLIVE, TOMATO AND COURGETTE TART

Puff pastry is notoriously difficult to make. I haven't dared making it from scratch yet but shop-bought works perfectly. This tart is great as a lunch option for friends at the weekend, served with some salad, or as a quick and easy midweek feast with plenty of leftovers for lunch the next day.

Serves 6

100g black olives, pitted

1 x 25g tin anchovies, drained

1 tbsp capers, drained

1 tsp Dijon mustard

1 tsp fresh lemon juice

4 tbsp extra-virgin olive oil

1 roll ready-to-use puff pastry

10 cherry tomatoes, halved

1 courgette, ribboned

1 log goat's cheese, sliced into rounds

1 egg, beaten

1 Preheat the oven to 200°C/180°C Fan/400°F.

2 For the tapenade: blend the olives, anchovies, capers, mustard and lemon juice in a food processor or a large jug if using a hand-held blender. Blitz until a rough paste is formed; slowly add the olive oil as you keep blending.

3 Gently roll the pastry from the packet onto a large rectangular baking tray.

4 Spread the tapenade evenly over the pastry leaving a 2cm border to allow the pastry to rise. Scatter the tomatoes, courgette and cheese on top.

5 Brush the pastry border with the beaten egg.

6 Bake in the oven for 20 minutes or until the pastry is golden.

7 Allow to cool for a few minutes before slicing and serving.

Variation

Butternut Squash, Walnut, Feta and Pesto Tart

3 tbsp pesto (see page 82), 2 tbsp cream cheese/crème fraîche/plain yoghurt, 80g thinly sliced butternut squash, 20g sliced red onion, 50g cubed feta cheese, 20g walnuts, 2 tsp honey

1 Mix the pesto and cream cheese together until smooth before spreading evenly over the puff pastry.
2 Scatter over the butternut squash, red onion and feta.
3 Bake in the oven for 15 minutes. Remove from the oven, add the walnuts and drizzle over the honey.
4 Return to oven and bake for a further 5 minutes or until the pastry is golden and the squash is cooked through.

RED PEPPER, SPINACH AND BRIE FRITTATA

Frittatas are just magic when you're starving and short on time. I also love them after a tough training or gym session as eggs are one of the best natural protein sources.

This recipe is brilliant for using up any leftover vegetables or meat in your fridge.

Serves 2

100g turnip, peeled and cubed
Coconut oil
½ medium red onion, thinly sliced
¼ red pepper, thinly sliced
3 fistfuls of spinach
2 tsp garlic butter (or 1 garlic clove, minced and 2 tsp butter)
2 eggs
2 tbsp milk
Freshly ground black pepper
50g brie, cubed
4 tbsp crème fraîche
1 tbsp pesto (see page 82)

1 Bring a pan of water to the boil. Add the turnip, cover and remove from the heat. Blanch for 10 minutes or until tender. Strain and rinse the turnip under cold running water until fully cool and set aside for later.

2 Melt 1 teaspoon of coconut oil in a heatproof frying pan.

3 Add the red onion and pepper to the pan and sauté until the onion has softened. Remove from the pan and set aside.

4 Add the cooled turnip, spinach and garlic butter to the pan and toss until well coated.

5 Continue to cook until the spinach wilts, return the onion and pepper to the pan.

6 Beat the eggs and milk together and season with pepper. Pour over the vegetable mixture and cook for 2 minutes.

7 Sprinkle the brie over the vegetables before placing under a grill for 5 minutes to cook through and crisp the eggs.

8 Whisk together the crème fraîche and pesto and serve on the side.

Handy hint!

If the handle of your frying pan isn't heatproof just cover with tin-foil to prevent it melting.

CREAMY APRICOT AND ALMOND TURKEY

Turkey is something a lot of people only eat once a year at Christmas. However, it is a great source of low-fat protein, which is good for building muscle and maintaining a steady weight.

This dish is heart-warming, with its mix of spices, and is really quick to prepare and cook. Chicken or lamb would also work well in this dish.

Serves 4

1 tsp coconut oil
400g turkey breast, sliced
1 small onion, thinly sliced
½ tsp ground turmeric
½ tsp ground cinnamon
100g crème fraîche
275ml milk
150g dried apricots, halved
50g raisins
25g flaked almonds

1 Melt the coconut oil over a medium heat in a large frying pan. Add the turkey and brown on all sides for about 10 minutes.
2 Add the onion, turmeric and cinnamon and continue to cook for 3–4 minutes until the turkey is cooked through.
3 Stir in the crème fraîche, milk, apricots, raisins and almonds until the crème fraîche has dissolved. Cook over a low heat for 8–10 minutes until the sauce thickens.
4 Serve with a grain of your choice or steamed greens.

CRISPY FISH TACOS

Everybody loves crispy fish and the secret is in the batter. This recipe uses rice flour, which forms the lightest tempura-style batter while also being naturally gluten-free. Any type of meaty white fish would work well. Increase the amount of paprika to spice things up a little.

Serves 4, makes 8 tacos

2 eggs

6 tbsp rice flour/plain white flour

4 tsp paprika

½ tsp sea-salt and freshly ground pepper

2 cod fillets, de-skinned and boned

½ red cabbage, thinly sliced

2 medium carrots, coarsely grated

Juice of ½ lemon

3 tsp honey

2 tbsp extra-virgin olive oil

4 tbsp cider vinegar

4 tbsp coconut oil

8 taco shells

4 tbsp crème fraîche

1 Whisk the eggs lightly in one bowl.

2 In another bowl, mix together the flour, paprika, salt and pepper.

3 Slice the cod fillets into goujons.

4 To batter the cod: simply dip one goujon at a time into the egg mix, then roll in the flour mix and leave to rest on a plate. Repeat with the remaining fish and place in the fridge until ready to cook.

5 For the slaw: mix the sliced red cabbage and grated carrots together. Add the lemon juice, honey, olive oil and vinegar and mix thoroughly to coat the slaw.

6 Melt the coconut oil in a non-stick pan over a medium heat. Add the fish goujons and cook for 5–8 minutes until golden on all sides.

7 Transfer the fish from the pan with a slotted spoon or spatula to a plate lined with kitchen paper to drain any excess oil.

8 Cook the taco shells as per packet instructions.

9 Stuff the tacos with the red cabbage slaw, place the cod goujons on top and a drizzle of crème fraîche.

SQUASH NOODLES WITH GARLIC PRAWNS

A ready-in-minutes dinner option, this is a light and filling meal. Make the most of butternut squash during summer and autumn when it's in season and at its best. Chicken or pork can easily replace the prawns.

Serves 2

½ butternut squash, spiralised or julienned
Coconut oil
2 cloves of garlic, minced
100g frozen cooked prawns, defrosted
8 cherry tomatoes, quartered
6 tbsp cottage cheese
2 tsp fresh lemon juice
100g rocket and spinach
2 tbsp dukkah (see page 85)

1 Bring a saucepan of water to the boil, add the butternut squash, remove from the heat, cover and blanch for 5 minutes. Drain and cool under a running cold tap until fully cooled.

2 Place 1 teaspoon of coconut oil in a large frying pan and melt over a medium heat, add the garlic and gently fry. Add the prawns and coat in the garlic.

3 Add the cherry tomatoes and butternut squash to the pan and cook together for 3 minutes.

4 Stir in the cottage cheese and lemon juice until well combined.

5 Create a bed of rocket and spinach on two plates, divide the prawn mixture and sprinkle over the dukkah.

Variations

- Replace the butternut squash with carrot, turnip, courgette, sweet potato, pumpkin or regular noodles as you like.
- For a veggie option, replace the prawns with sliced aubergine rounds.

Snacks

When You Need a Boost

Buckwheat and Coconut Prune Bars   178

Sweet Potato Toasts   180

My Favourite Snacks   182

Vietnamese Rice Paper Rolls   184

BUCKWHEAT AND COCONUT PRUNE BARS

These bars are perfect when you want something healthy but sweet. I normally make a batch of them and pop them in the freezer once cooled for those exact moments.

Makes 12 bars

70g prunes, stoned
2 tbsp coconut oil, melted
2 tbsp nut butter
1 egg white
35g Brazil nuts
30g pistachio nuts
20g walnuts
2 tbsp sunflower seeds
2 tbsp pumpkin seeds
1 tbsp poppy seeds
2 tbsp cranberries
2 tsp desiccated coconut
1 tsp raw buckwheat groats

1 Preheat the oven to 180°C/160°C Fan/350°F and line a 21cm square baking tray with parchment.
2 Place the prunes in a bowl and cover with boiling hot water to soften for 5 minutes.
3 Once the prunes are softened, blend in a food processor with the coconut oil and nut butter until smooth.
4 Whisk the egg white until fluffy peaks form.
5 Blitz or finely chop all the nuts together to form a coarse mix.
6 In a large bowl, place the nuts, seeds, cranberries and prune mix. Stir through the egg white until well combined.
7 Pour into the lined baking tray; flatten with the back of a spoon before sprinkling over the desiccated coconut and buckwheat groats.
8 Bake in the oven for 20 minutes; allow to cool fully on a wire rack before cutting into bars.
9 Store in an airtight container or freeze.

Variation

For a nut-free option: swap the nut butter for tahini, and the Brazil nuts, pistachios and walnuts for 80g mixed seeds.

SWEET POTATO TOASTS

These toasts are the ultimate solution when you don't know what you want to eat but you want it now! The microwave is your best friend here to bake the sweet potato in no time and to ensure you keep that hunger at bay. The sweet potato can obviously be replaced with a bread of your choice.

Sweet Potato
Serves 1

½ medium sweet potato

1 Preheat the oven to 200°C/180°C Fan/400°F.
2 Bake the sweet potato whole in the oven for 20 minutes until soft through or cook in the microwave at the highest heat setting for 3 minutes.
3 Cut into thick slices and layer with your choice of toppings.

My favourite toppings:

- Cottage cheese, cooked beetroot slices and tahini drizzle
- Crème fraîche, roasted tomato and pesto
- Mashed avocado and dukkah
- Crème fraîche, smoked salmon and cucumber curls
- Almond nut butter, banana slices and dark chocolate chips

MY FAVOURITE SNACKS

A selection of my go-to snacks for any time of the day, but usually for my morning break in work or before training.

FRUIT AND YOGHURT WITH SEED SPRINKLE

Serves 1

70g plain yoghurt
Chopped fruit of your choice
2 tbsp milled linseed
1 tbsp pumpkin seeds
1 tbsp sunflower seeds

1 Layer a glass or jar with yoghurt and fruit.
2 Sprinkle over the seed mix.

APPLE WITH NUT BUTTER

Serves 1

1 apple, cored and cut into round slices
1 tbsp fresh lemon juice
2 tbsp almond nut butter (see page 88)

1 Roll the apple slices in the lemon juice to prevent them browning.
2 Top the apple slices with the nut butter.

VEG STICKS AND HUMMUS

Serves 1

1 carrot/2 celery sticks/¼ cucumber/
    ¼ red pepper, cut into match sticks
4 tbsp hummus (see page 80)

1 Place the hummus in a jar or re-sealable container and dip the vegetable sticks in.

NUTS

The easiest snack option as no preparation or cleaning is required and nuts are bursting with essential protein, fatty acids and minerals. The main thing to remember is portion size, as half a bag can disappear before you know it. For nut butter, 2 tablespoons is one portion.

SMOKED MACKEREL CRUSH
Serves 6

2 smoked mackerel fillets
3 spring onions, thinly sliced
3 tbsp Greek-style yoghurt or crème fraîche
1 tbsp fresh lemon juice

1   Using a fork, flake the mackerel fillets into a bowl, ensuring to remove any bones or skin.
2   Add the spring onions, yoghurt and lemon juice to the mackerel and stir together.
3   Keeps fresh in the fridge for up to 3 days.
4   To serve: spread on a slice of my Oat and Seed Yoghurt Loaf (see page 56).

VIETNAMESE RICE PAPER ROLLS

Rice paper rolls are staples in every restaurant and café in Vietnam. Traditionally served with a sweet chilli or peanut satay sauce, I find they also work great with hummus. Rice paper is a great substitute for typical wraps or tortillas, which means these rolls work great as lunchbox fillers and are perfectly light and fresh.

Fill them as you like with vegetables, meat, fish and even fruit. My favourite fillings are hot smoked salmon and prawns. You can also exclude the rice paper and just fill the baby gem leaves.

Rolling can be a little tricky so take your time. The main thing to remember is less is more with your filling to ensure the rice paper doesn't rip.

Makes 12 rolls

170g tinned salmon/mackerel/
   12 cooked whole prawns
1 head baby gem lettuce,
   washed and leaves separated
100g beansprouts
½ cucumber, halved, cored and
   thinly sliced
1 carrot, coarsely grated
12 dried rice paper wrappers
   (20cm in diameter)
500ml hot water
1 tbsp fresh mint/coriander,
   finely chopped
Sweet chilli sauce (see page 86)
2 tbsp crunchy peanut or
   almond butter
1 tsp coconut oil, melted
½ tsp paprika

1. Drain and flake the fish from the tin or deshell the prawns.
2. Place each fish and vegetable ingredient in individual bowls.
3. Place the hot water in a shallow frying pan.
4. Dip one rice paper wrapper into the water until it begins to soften (about 30 seconds). Remove, shake off any excess water and place on a dry surface like a chopping board.
5. Place a lettuce leaf on the wrapper close to the edge nearest you, add some beansprouts, cucumber, carrot, 1 tablespoon fish and a sprinkle of mint or coriander (less is more as you don't want the wrapper to burst if too full).
6. Fold the closest edge of the wrapper over the filling, then fold in the sides and roll up tightly to complete the folding like you would roll a burrito or wrap.
7. Set aside and repeat with the remaining wrappers and filling.
8. For the nut sauce: mix the nut butter, melted coconut oil and paprika together until well combined.
9. Serve with a choice of sauces.

Handy hint!

Source rice paper wrappers in your local Asian store or larger supermarkets.

Where Healthy and Decadence Collide

White Chocolate and Raspberry Cheesecake — 188

Date Caramel Banoffee Pie — 190

Avocado and Raspberry Mousse Cups — 192

Dark Chocolate Beetroot Cake — 194

Strawberry and Ginger Yoghurt Cups — 196

Roast Honey Fruits — 198

Meringue Kisses — 200

Apple, Pear and Ginger Crumble — 202

Coconut and Berry Sponge Cake — 204

WHITE CHOCOLATE AND RASPBERRY CHEESECAKE

This is a special-occasion cake, perfect for a birthday, celebration dinner or at Christmas. I haven't produced it yet for family, friends or colleagues who didn't literally lick the plates clean.

Serves 8

200g Oreo-style cookies
50g butter
300g white chocolate
75g caster sugar
400g cream cheese
Zest and juice of ½ a lemon
300ml cream
200g raspberries

For the base:
1 Remove and discard the centre of the Oreo-style cookies and crush until they resemble fine breadcrumbs.
2 Melt the butter and stir through the crushed biscuits. Press into the bottom of a 20cm spring form tin and place in the fridge for 10 minutes.

For the filling:
1 Melt the white chocolate in a heatproof bowl over a simmering pan of water.
2 Using a hand-held beater blend together the cream cheese, lemon juice, zest and caster sugar until smooth.
3 In a separate bowl, stiffly whip the cream.
4 Whisk the melted chocolate into the cream cheese, followed by the whipped cream until well combined.

To assemble:
1 Scatter half the raspberries over the biscuit base, followed by half the filling. Scatter over the remaining raspberries and finish with the remaining filling.
2 Place in the fridge for at least 2 hours to ensure fully set.

DATE CARAMEL BANOFFEE PIE

I love the combination of smooth caramel with fresh banana in banoffee pie. I have used dates to create a refined-sugar-free caramel. This caramel is one of my favourite things to make as it is so versatile and can be served heated with ice cream and some nuts for a really quick and easy dessert.

Serves 8

For the caramel:
250g dates, pitted
1 tsp bread soda
2 overripe bananas
6 tbsp boiling hot water
3 tbsp coconut oil, melted
2 tbsp nut butter

For the base:
180g almonds
5 tbsp oat flour
6 tbsp coconut oil, melted

For the topping:
3 tbsp crème fraîche
70 ml cream
1 bar dark chocolate
2 fresh bananas
1 tsp lemon juice

1 Place the dates and baking soda in a bowl and cover with boiling water to soften.

For the base:
1 Place the almonds in a roasting tin and gently roast at 180°C/160°C Fan/350°F for 20 minutes.
2 Blitz them until coarse using a food processor at the highest setting; you will have to scrape down the sides on numerous occasions.
3 Combine the blitzed almonds with the oat flour and coconut oil.
4 Press into the base and sides of a 20cm-round loose-bottomed fluted tin. Place in the fridge for at least 30 minutes.

For the caramel:
1 Drain the dates and place in a food processor with the bananas, boiling water and coconut oil. Blitz until smooth. Add in the nut butter and blitz again until smooth.
2 Spoon the caramel onto the almond base and place in the fridge.

To assemble:
1 Whip the crème fraiche and cream together until soft peaks form.
2 Make the chocolate curls (see facing page).
3 Cut the fresh bananas into rounds, mix through the lemon juice to prevent browning, and layer over the caramel.
4 Finish by evenly spreading the whipped cream on top and sprinkling with the chocolate curls.

For the chocolate curls:

1 Place the bar of chocolate on a flat surface, smooth side up and with one edge resting against your stomach. Protect your clothes with a clean tea towel.

2 Take the blade of a long knife and place it at the opposite end of the chocolate bar. Scrape the knife carefully along the top of the bar towards you, forming curls with the blade.

3 Repeat until you have created enough to cover the cake.

AVOCADO AND RASPBERRY MOUSSE CUPS

These are irresistible little cups of silky smooth mousse. You won't even realise there's avocado in them, so they're perfect for fussy eaters.

Makes 3

50g hazelnuts
2 ripe avocados
2 tbsp honey
½ tsp vanilla extract
2 tbsp raw cacao powder
2 tbsp fresh raspberries

1 Toast the hazelnuts in a dry frying pan over a medium heat until the shells begin to loosen.
2 Remove from the heat and allow to cool fully before roughly chopping or blitzing in a food processor.

For the mousse:
1 Scoop the avocado flesh from the shell and blitz in a food processor with the honey and vanilla extract until smooth.
2 Add the cacao powder and 1 tablespoon of raspberries and blitz again until well combined.
3 Place in the fridge until ready to use.

To serve:
1 Divide the mousse into small bowls, glass tumblers or jars.
2 Scatter over the crushed nuts and remaining raspberries.

Variation

Dark Chocolate and Orange
Replace the vanilla extract and raspberries with 2 tbsp fresh orange juice and 2 tsp orange zest.

DARK CHOCOLATE BEETROOT CAKE

I never thought a vegetable could taste so good until I had my first bite of a chocolate beetroot cake!

Raw or pre-cooked beetroot works well in this recipe. Just make sure to wear gloves when grating, otherwise you will have pink hands for days!

I find the cake tastes even better the following day. Why not prepare it in advance, store in the fridge and add the icing just before serving?

Serves 12

260g dark chocolate

6 eggs, separated

400g beetroot, raw or
 pre-cooked, grated

4 tbsp honey

1 heaped tsp vanilla extract

160g ground almonds

1 heaped tsp baking powder

1 tbsp raw cacao powder

For the top:

150g crème fraîche

3 tbsp beetroot juice (reserved
 from the grated beetroot)

1 tsp honey

Dark chocolate curls

1 tbsp grated beetroot

2 tbsp flaked almonds

1 Grease a 23cm round cake tin with oil. Line the base with parchment and lightly dust the sides with flour. Preheat the oven to 180°C/160°C Fan/350°F.

2 Melt the dark chocolate in a heatproof bowl over a pan of simmering water.

3 In a large mixing bowl, whisk the egg yolks together and stir through the grated beetroot.

4 Once the chocolate has melted, add to the beetroot with the honey and vanilla.

5 Sift in the ground almonds, baking powder and raw cacao to the beetroot until well combined.

6 Use an electric beater to whip the egg whites together until stiff peaks form (they should stick to the beater when held upside down).

7 Gradually fold the egg whites through the mix with a spatula until fully combined.

8 Pour the mix into the prepared cake tin. Tap the base of the tin on the worktop a few times to release any air bubbles.

9 Place in the oven and bake for 35–40 minutes or until a skewer comes out cleanly.

10 Remove from the oven and allow to cool in the tin.

11 Once cooled, carefully remove from the tin and either store in the fridge in an airtight container or cover with the icing and serve.

Handy hints!

- Check out my Date Caramel Banoffee Pie recipe on page 191 for how to make chocolate curls.
- The cake will keep fresh in the fridge for up to 4 days.

To assemble:
1 Whisk the crème fraîche, beetroot juice and honey together by hand until smooth to form a rich pink colour.
2 Spread a generous layer of icing over the top of the cake.
3 Decorate by scattering the flaked almonds, chocolate curls and grated beetroot over the top.

STRAWBERRY AND GINGER YOGHURT CUPS

Strawberries to me signify summer: long days filled with sunshine, fresh air and eating outdoors. This recipe is perfect as a light dessert option, and can be made in advance and kept in the fridge until ready to serve.

Serves 4

10 gingernut biscuits
25g butter/ 3 tbsp coconut oil, melted
150g crème fraîche
200g Greek-style yoghurt
Zest of ½ a lemon
250g fresh strawberries, sliced

1 Place the biscuits in a bag and crush with a rolling pin or place in a food processor and blitz until a crumble consistency is formed. Combine the biscuits and melted butter in a bowl until well mixed.
2 In a separate mixing bowl, combine the crème fraîche, yoghurt and lemon zest.

To assemble:
1 Divide the crushed biscuits amongst the glasses and press down firmly into the base.
2 Place the sliced strawberries around the outside of the glasses and spoon in the yoghurt mix.
3 Top with some more strawberries, a sprinkle of the crushed biscuits and lemon zest.
4 Place in the fridge until ready to serve.

ROAST HONEY FRUITS

Any stoned or cored fruits work well in this dessert, which makes a quick and easy treat to finish off a meal. A spoon of vanilla ice cream on top would also be delish!

Serves 4

2 pears, halved and cored

2 plums, halved and stoned

2 tsp honey

4 tsp granola (see page 30)

4 tbsp plain yoghurt

1 Preheat the oven to 180°C/160°C Fan/350°F.

2 Place all the fruit skin side down on a baking tray or ovenproof dish.

3 Drizzle the honey over the fruits and bake in the oven for 20 minutes or until soft.

To serve:

1 Divide the fruit amongst the plates.

2 Place one tablespoon of yoghurt into the centre of the fruit and sprinkle the granola on top.

MERINGUE KISSES

This is a showstopper dessert that I promise is really easy to make!

The secret is heating the sugar before making the meringue, which creates a very soft marshmallow effect when you bite in. You can also prepare the meringues in advance and keep them fresh in an airtight container for up to two weeks.

Makes 15 kisses, 30 meringue shells

300g caster sugar
5 egg whites
50g dark chocolate

For the filling:
200ml cream
2 tablespoons fresh raspberries
3 tbsp pistachio nuts

1. Preheat the oven to 220°C/200°C Fan/425°F. Line two rectangular baking trays with parchment.
2. Pour all the caster sugar into one lined baking tray and heat in the oven for 7 minutes.
3. In a clean bowl, beat the egg whites until stiff peaks form.
4. Remove the sugar from the oven and reduce the heat to 120°C/100°C Fan/250°F – keep the door ajar with a wooden spoon to speed up this process.
5. Gradually add the sugar to the egg whites whilst continuing to beat until glossy stiff peaks form and the sugar is fully incorporated.
6. Use a piping bag to pipe out kisses on the lined baking trays. Keep the bag tight, straight and directly above the baking tray. Squeeze from a 2cm height from the baking tray and then let go before pulling up to form the peak. You can also make kisses by adding heaped tablespoons of the mixture and then pulling up from the centre to create a peak.
7. Place in the oven and bake for 40 minutes or until the meringues easily peel off the parchment. Allow to cool in the oven with the door held slightly open with a wooden spoon.
8. Once the meringues are cooled, melt the dark chocolate in a heatproof bowl over a pan of simmering water.
9. Dip the base of half the meringues in the chocolate and place on their side to set on parchment.

For the filling:

1 Whip the cream until soft peaks form.
2 Divide the cream between two bowls. Mash half the raspberries and add to one bowl of cream, combine well until you get an even pink colour.
3 Blitz the pistachios in a food processor or else place in a resealable bag and crush with a rolling pin until you get a crumble consistency.

To assemble:

1 Mix and match the cream, fresh raspberries and pistachios as you like until all are filled.
2 Keep fresh in the fridge before serving.

APPLE, PEAR AND GINGER CRUMBLE

There is something so comforting about crumble. It is a great dessert at any time of the year – just add in whatever berries or fruit are in season. Ginger is one of my favourite spices as it is brilliant for our immune systems to ward off flus and colds. Serve with some vanilla ice cream, crème fraîche or plain yoghurt.

Serves 6

4 pears, peeled and cored

5 apples, peeled and cored

2 inch piece of fresh peeled ginger, grated

5 tbsp jumbo oats

3 tbsp pumpkin and sunflower seeds

3 tbsp flaked almonds

2 tbsp desiccated coconut

2 tbsp ground linseed

8 dates, pitted and chopped

3 tbsp coconut oil, solid

1 Roughly cube the pears and apples and place in a saucepan. Add the grated ginger and just enough water to cover the fruit.

2 Bring the fruit to a boil, reduce the heat to a simmer and continue to cook until the fruit has begun to soften.

3 Place all the remaining ingredients in a bowl and rub through the coconut oil with your fingertips until a crumble is formed.

4 Transfer the cooked fruit to a heatproof dish or small individual ramekins.

5 Cover with the oat crumble and bake in the oven at 180°C/160°C Fan/350°F for 30 minutes or until golden.

COCONUT AND BERRY SPONGE CAKE

This is a real crowd pleaser – what more could you want from a cake than fluffy, light sponge, fresh cream and berries? The best bit is it's gluten-free too so perfect for anyone with an intolerance, of which there can be many when you're baking for a group.

Serves 8

100g caster sugar

150g unsalted butter, softened

3 eggs, lightly beaten

125g gluten-free or plain flour

25g coconut flour/105g plain flour

1 tsp baking powder

80g crème fraîche

1 tbsp milk

2 tbsp fresh lemon juice

For the topping:

80g crème fraîche

4 tbsp Greek-style plain yoghurt

1 tbsp honey

2 tbsp raspberry jam

200g fresh berries

1 Preheat the oven to 180°C/160°C Fan/350°F, line and grease two 20cm round loose bottomed baking tins.

2 Cream the sugar and butter together until light and fluffy with a hand-held or stand electric kitchen mixer.

3 With the motor running, gradually add 1 tablespoon of the beaten eggs at a time until well combined.

4 Add in the dry ingredients and beat well.

5 Fold in the crème fraîche and milk by hand; followed by the lemon juice and continue to fold.

6 Divide the mixture between the two prepared tins and bake in the oven for 15 minutes. Increase the oven to 200°C/180°C Fan/400°F and bake for 15–20 minutes or until a skewer come out clean.

7 Remove from the oven and allow to cool in the tin.

For the topping:

1 Beat the crème fraîche and yoghurt together until smooth.

2 Add in the honey and continue to beat until thick and creamy. Chill in the fridge.

To assemble:

1 Remove the cooled cakes from the tins and spread a thin layer of jam over the surface followed by the topping and stack on top of each other.

2 Top with the berries and enjoy.

REFERENCES

Freezing Food   Page 14
www.safefood.eu/Food-Safety/Chill/Chilling.aspx

Defrosting food   Page 15
www.fsai.ie/faq/domestic.html

Athlete Plate   Pages 17, 18, 19, 20
www.teamusa.org/About-the-USOC/Athelete-Development/
Sport-Performance/Nutrtion/Athlete-Factsheets-and-Resources

Exercise Guidelines   Page 21
www.who.int/dietphysicalactivity/factsheet_recommendations/en/

Oat and Berry Recharger   Page 42
www.indi.ie/images/public_docs/25_INDI_Book_(Sport).pdf

ACKNOWLEDGEMENTS

Main Photography by:
Pages ii–iii, vi, 2–4, 13, 16, 23, 27–28, 31–37, 41–49, 59–63, 67–69, 73, 77, 81–83, 90–93, 97, 103, 107–108, 117–121, 127–129, 134–155, 159, 163–176, 181–183, 186, 191–193, 199, 205, 210: © Aidan Crawley.

Pages 11, 25, 39, 51, 53–57, 65, 71, 75, 89, 95, 99, 101, 105, 111–115, 124–125, 131–133, 157, 161, 179, 185, 189, 195–197, 201–203, and the cover image: © Jennifer Oppermann.

Additional photographs supplied by:
Pages 5, 7: Peter Hickey, GAA Pics, © GAA Pics.

Pages 6, 8: © Sportsfile

Pages 19–20: thanks to the United States Olympic Committee Sport Dieticians and the University of Colorado (UCCS) Sport Nutrition Graduate Program alongside Dr Nanna Meyer for allowing reproduction of the Athlete Plate.

Page 22: © Sarah Casey

Page 78: © Sinéad Delahunty

Food preparation and styling by Sinéad Delahunty.

Props: sourced with thanks from Avoca, The Props Library and private collections of the author's own, friends and family.

Ingredients kindly provided by Lidl Ireland (excluding ethnic ingredients), The Bretzel Bakery (sourdough bread) and Glenisk (yoghurt, milk, crème fraîche and cream).

CONVERTING INGREDIENT QUANTITIES

As mentioned for consistency, I would suggest always using the same teaspoon or tablespoon in your cutlery drawer. If you want to weigh out these measurements, 1 teaspoon = 5ml and 1 tablespoon = 15ml.

Another top tip is that ml = g. This is very useful when measuring liquid quantities as it can be really difficult to tell the exact quantity of a measuring jug.

For dimensions: 1 inch = 2.5cm and 2 inches = 5cm.

Ounces to Grams	
Ounces	Grams
½ oz	10g
¾ oz	20g
1 oz	25g
1½ oz	40g
2 oz	50g
2½ oz	60g
3 oz	75g
4 oz	110g
4½ oz	125g
5 oz	150g
6 oz	175g
8 oz	200g
9 oz	250g
10 oz	275g
10½ oz	300g
14 oz	400g
1lb 1½ oz	500g
1 lb 5 oz	600g

Pints to Litres	
Imperial	Metric
1 fl oz	25ml
2 fl oz	50ml
4 fl oz	100ml
6 fl oz	175ml
7 fl oz	200ml
8 fl oz	225ml
8½ fl oz	250ml
10 fl oz	300ml
15 fl oz	450ml
17 fl oz	500ml
1⅓ pt (25½ fl oz)	750ml
1¾ pt (35 fl oz)	1 litre

Liquid Conversions		
American	Imperial	Metric
1 tbsp	½ fl oz	15ml
⅛ cup	1 fl oz	30ml
¼ cup	2 fl oz	60ml
½ cup	4 fl oz	120ml
1 cup	8 fl oz	240ml
1 pint	16 fl oz	480ml

THANK YOU

I could fill this entire book with just thank-yous! One for each person that has helped me reach this point not only with my blog and this book but throughout life. I will more than likely leave someone out but here's my best shot!

Firstly to my family, Mam, Dad and brothers Eoin and Brian – I don't know where I would be without you all. Thank you for the endless support and advice, the kick up the backside when it's needed and the grounding back to normality when sometimes I think I'm better than I am. A very special word of thanks to my amazing mam, Mary! I honestly don't know how I would get through life without you helping me every step of the way. Thank you for everything, you all mean the world to me!

To all the team at The Collins Press, who have worked tirelessly on this project, guiding, reviewing and constantly steering me in the right direction. I really appreciate it and the finished book is the result of all your hard work.

To Aidan Crawley and Jennifer Oppermann, the people behind the cameras. Thank you for waiting patiently for all the dishes to be prepared, witnessing one or two kitchen disasters along the way, dealing masterfully with my pedantic requests and being a source of great advice and encouragement. Special thanks to Jennifer who brought such love and care to this book.

To Lidl, Glenisk, Avoca and The Bretzel Bakery, thank you for all the support and encouragement throughout the book's development and launch; your input was vital and really appreciated.

To Ann Harte, Ann Horan and Catherine Ryan for sharing your private crockery collections with me – I am forever indebted to you all!

To the WGPA for selecting me to be included in the Athlete Mentorship programme and matching me with Marian Byrne. Marian was my sounding board throughout the entire publication process – constantly offering her wisdom and support not only about the book but about life in general, I couldn't have done it without you!

To all my current and former teammates – thank you for being amazing friends and comrades in arms on the field and especially for all the constant support and taste-testing off the field.

To all my colleagues in Connolly Hospital, Blanchardstown – some of you are my toughest taste-testers and biggest fans so thank you for all the support, feedback and friendships.

To all my friends near and far, thank you for always understanding, bringing a smile to my face and just being you – here's to many more great nights out, dinner party extravaganzas, adventures and chats; you are all the best! Special thanks to my three besties – Jenny, Sarah and Katie! Not only for your help with this book – recipe testing, brainstorming, proofing and

picture choosing, but for the endless friendship and laughs you all provide daily. Here's to many more!

Last but not least, my *Delalicious* fans – without you this book wouldn't be here! As you know, the blog started out small and has blossomed in no small part due to all your interest and support. Thank you for reading and recreating my recipes. My only wish is that you continue to follow the blog and try every recipe in this book as they have been lovingly selected just for you!

Happy cooking and go raibh míle maith agaibh,

Sinéad

INDEX

almond coins, 62

almonds
  almond coins, 62
  apple with nut butter, 182
  banana and nut butter smoothie, 42
  bircher muesli, 32
  broccoli and almond turmeric grains, 130
  creamy apricot and almond turkey, 170
  granola, 30
  homemade nut butter, 88
  potato salad with beetroot and almond, 112
  raspberry and almond coins, 62

apples
  apple and cinnamon muesli, 32
  apple, pear and ginger crumble, 202
  apple with nut butter, 182
  flu-fighter juice, 40
  green-eyed monster juice, 40
  oat and berry recharger, 42

apricots
  apricot and pecan flapjacks, 64
  creamy apricot and almond turkey, 170

Athlete Plate, 12, 17–20

avocados
  avocado and raspberry mousse cups, 192
  ginger bug juice, 40
  guacamole, 87

babhka rolls, 74–5

bacon
  bacon and balsamic roasted tomato
    flatbreads, 38
  pea, spinach and smoked bacon soup, 96
  smoky baked beans with bacon and
    sourdough, 44

baked beans see beans

baked cod with nettle pesto and cherry tomatoes,
  140

baking see breads; cakes and biscuits; scones

bananas
  banana and nut butter smoothie, 42
  banana and oat pancakes, 48
  dark chocolate and walnut banana bread, 70
  date caramel banoffee pie, 190
  quinoa and oat banana bake, 36

basil and sunflower seed pesto, 84

beans
  beetroot and mint hummus, 80
  beetroot, feta and black bean burgers, 162
  burrito beef bowl with Mexican bean
    salsa, 146
  cashew and dark chocolate bites, 76
  chicken and beans, 136
  smoky baked beans with bacon and
    sourdough, 44
  white chocolate and raspberry bites, 76
  see also green beans

beef
  beef steak with salsa verde and rainbow
    chips, 156
  burrito beef bowl with Mexican bean salsa,
    146

beetroot
  beetroot and carrot soup, 104
  beetroot and mint hummus, 80
  beetroot and mozzarella stacks, 123
  beetroot, feta and black bean burgers, 162
  beetroot, freekeh, cucumber and mackerel
    salad, 120
  bulgur wheat, quinoa and beetroot risotto, 160
  dark chocolate beetroot cake, 194–5
  flu-fighter juice, 40
  potato salad with beetroot and almond, 112

berries
  avocado and raspberry mousse cups, 192
  berry and oat muffins, 68
  berry scones, 58
  coconut and berry sponge cake, 204
  meringue kisses, 200–201
  oat and berry recharger, 42
  raspberry and almond coins, 62
  strawberry and ginger yoghurt cups, 196
  white chocolate and raspberry bites, 76
  white chocolate and raspberry cheesecake,
    188

berry and oat muffins, 68

berry scones, 58
bircher muesli, 32
biscuits *see* cakes and biscuits
black beans *see* beans
blenders, 24
blueberries *see* berries
breads
    dark chocolate and walnut banana bread, 70
    flatbreads, 38
    Mediterranean style loaf, 56
    oat and seed yoghurt loaf, 56
    spelt babhka rolls, 74–5
breakfasts
    bacon and balsamic roasted tomato
        flatbreads, 38
    bircher muesli, 32
    carrot, courgette and corn fritters, 50
    crunchy date and seed plum pots, 52
    cupcake quiches, 34
    granola, 30
    juices, 40
    oat and berry recharger, 42
    pancakes, 46–8
    quinoa and oat banana bake, 36
    smoky baked beans with bacon and
        sourdough, 44
brie *see* cheese
broccoli
    broccoli and almond turmeric grains, 130
    broccoli, feta, tomato and hazelnut salad, 122
    citrus chicken with broccoli rice, 152
    creamy broccoli and cashew soup, 100
    tender-stem broccoli, spinach, baby gem and
        vegetable crisps, 118
buckwheat
    buckwheat and coconut prune bars, 178
    buckwheat pancakes, 46
bulgur wheat *see also* grains
    bulgur wheat, quinoa and beetroot risotto, 160
burgers
    beetroot, feta and black bean burgers, 162
    millet, butternut squash and linseed burgers,
        158–9
burrito beef bowl with Mexican bean salsa, 146
butter beans *see* beans

butternut squash
    butternut squash, walnut, feta and pesto tart,
        167
    kale, roast butternut squash, quinoa
        and pomegranate salad, 126
    millet, butternut squash and linseed burgers,
        158–9
    spiced butternut squash soup, 98
    squash noodles with garlic prawns, 174

cabbage
    red cabbage, carrot and seed slaw, 113
cakes and biscuits
    almond coins, 62
    apricot and pecan flapjacks, 64
    berry and oat muffins, 68
    carrot cake with yoghurt icing, 72
    cashew and dark chocolate bites, 76
    coconut and berry sponge cake, 204
    dark chocolate beetroot cake, 194–5
    dark chocolate coins, 62
    fruit and nut dark chocolate oaties, 66
    raspberry and almond coins, 62
    white chocolate and raspberry bites, 76
    white chocolate and raspberry cheesecake,
        188
cannellini beans *see* beans
carrots
    beetroot and carrot soup, 104
    carrot and seed slaw, 122
    carrot cake with yoghurt icing, 72
    carrot, courgette and corn fritters, 50
    flu-fighter juice, 40
    rainbow chips, 156
    red cabbage, carrot and seed slaw, 113
    roast carrot and garlic hummus, 82
    roast root vegetable and coriander soup, 92
    roast vegetable and cranberry grains, 132
cashews
    cashew and dark chocolate bites, 76
    cashew sauce, 159
    coriander, cashew and walnut pesto, 83
    creamy broccoli and cashew soup, 100
    crispy Asian slaw with cod and roasted
        cashews, 128

cauliflower
    cauliflower tabbouleh, 110
    creamy roast cauliflower soup, 106
    roast vegetable and cranberry grains, 132
celery
    green-eyed monster juice, 40
charred baby gem, 112
cheese
    beetroot and mozzarella stacks, 123
    beetroot, feta and black bean burgers, 162
    broccoli, feta, tomato and hazelnut salad, 122
    butternut squash, walnut, feta and pesto tart,
       167
    goat's cheese, black olive, tomato and
       courgette tart, 166
    nettle and parmesan pesto, 84
    parmesan and garlic hummus, 80
    red pepper, spinach and brie frittata, 168
chicken
    chicken and beans, 136
    chicken and grain traybake, 142
    citrus chicken with broccoli rice, 152
    ginger, chicken and chickpea curry, 144
    Mediterranean quinoa and bulgur salad with
       shredded chicken, 116
chickpeas
    ginger, chicken and chickpea curry, 144
    parmesan and garlic hummus, 80
    roast carrot and garlic hummus, 82
    roast red pepper and smoked paprika
       hummus, 81
chocolate
    cashew and dark chocolate bites, 76
    dark chocolate and hazelnut babhka rolls,
       74–5
    dark chocolate and orange mousse cups, 192
    dark chocolate and walnut banana bread, 70
    dark chocolate beetroot cake, 194–5
    dark chocolate coins, 62
    fruit and nut dark chocolate oaties, 66
    meringue kisses, 200–201
    white chocolate and raspberry bites, 76
    white chocolate and raspberry cheesecake,
       188
chopping boards, 24
cinnamon and pecan babhka rolls, 74–5
citrus chicken with broccoli rice, 152

coconut
    apple, pear and ginger crumble, 202
    buckwheat and coconut prune bars, 178
    coconut and berry sponge cake, 204
    granola, 30
composting, 15
cookies see cakes and biscuits
coriander, cashew and walnut pesto, 83
corn
    carrot, courgette and corn fritters, 50
    Mexican bean salsa, 146
courgettes
    carrot, courgette and corn fritters, 50
    courgetti prawn, 138
    goat's cheese, black olive, tomato and
       courgette tart, 166
cranberries
    apricot and pecan flapjacks, 64
    Bircher muesli, 32
    fruit and nut dark chocolate oaties, 66
    granola, 30
    roast vegetable and cranberry grains, 132
creamy apricot and almond turkey, 170
creamy broccoli and cashew soup, 100
creamy fish pie, 148
creamy garlic mushroom sauce, 157
creamy roast cauliflower soup, 106
creamy tahini dressing, 87
crispy Asian slaw with cod and roasted cashews,
    128
crispy fish tacos, 172
crumbles
    apple, pear and ginger crumble, 202
crunchy date and seed plum pots, 52
cucumber
    beetroot, freekeh, cucumber and mackerel
       salad, 120
    green-eyed monster juice, 40
cupcake quiches, 34
curries
    ginger, chicken and chickpea curry, 144

dark chocolate and hazelnut babhka rolls, 74–5
dark chocolate and orange mousse cups, 192
dark chocolate and walnut banana bread, 70
dark chocolate beetroot cake, 194–5
dark chocolate coins, 62

dates
    crunchy date and seed plum pots, 52
    date caramel banoffee pie, 190–91
defrosting food, 15
Delalicious blog, 1, 8–10
desserts
    apple, pear and ginger crumble, 202
    avocado and raspberry mousse cups, 192
    coconut and berry sponge cake, 204
    dark chocolate and orange mousse cups, 192
    dark chocolate beetroot cake, 194–5
    date caramel banoffee pie, 190–91
    meringue kisses, 200–201
    roast honey fruits, 198
    strawberry and ginger yoghurt cups, 196
    white chocolate and raspberry cheesecake,
        188
dips *see* sauces, dressings and dips
dressings *see* sauces, dressings and dips
dukkah, 85

eating out, 12, 15
eggs
    cupcake quiches, 34
    red pepper, spinach and brie frittata, 168
exercise, 21

feta *see* cheese
Fish
    baked cod with nettle pesto and cherry
        tomatoes, 140
    beetroot, freekeh, cucumber and mackerel
        salad, 120
    creamy fish pie, 148
    crispy Asian slaw with cod and roasted
        cashews, 128
    crispy fish tacos, 172
    grilled salmon with pesto and roasted stuffed
        sweet potato, 154
    smoked mackerel crush, 183
    Vietnamese rice paper rolls, 184

flapjacks
    apricot and pecan flapjacks, 64
flatbreads, 38
flu-fighter juice, 40
fluffy oat scones, 60

food intolerances, 26
food philosophy, 10–12
food processors, 24
food shopping, 13, 15
food waste, 15
freekeh *see* grains
freezing food, 14, 15
Frenchie dressing, 86
frittatas
    red pepper, spinach and brie frittata, 168
fritters
    carrot, courgette and corn fritters, 50
fruit and nut dark chocolate oaties, 66
fruit and yoghurt with seed sprinkle, 182

Gaelic football, 4–8
ginger
    apple, pear and ginger crumble, 202
    ginger bug juice, 40
    ginger, chicken and chickpea curry, 144
    strawberry and ginger yoghurt cups, 196
goat's cheese, black olive, tomato and courgette
    tart, 166
grains
    beetroot, freekeh, cucumber and mackerel
        salad, 120
    broccoli and almond turmeric grains, 130
    bulgur wheat, quinoa and beetroot risotto, 160
    chicken and grain traybake, 142
    kale, roast butternut squash, quinoa and
        pomegranate salad, 126
    Mediterranean quinoa and bulgur salad with
        shredded chicken, 116
    millet, butternut squash and linseed burgers,
        158–9
    quinoa and oat banana bake, 36
    roast vegetable and cranberry grains, 132
granola, 30

green beans
    sticky sesame pork and greens, 150
green-eyed monster juice, 40
grilled salmon with pesto and roasted stuffed
    sweet potato, 154
Grow It Yourself website, 17
growing food, 17
guacamole, 87

hazelnuts
    broccoli, feta, tomato and hazelnut salad, 122
    dark chocolate and hazelnut babhka rolls,
       74–5
    dukkah, 85
    fruit and nut dark chocolate oaties, 66
homemade nut butter, 88
hummus
    beetroot and mint, 80
    parmesan and garlic, 80
    roast carrot and garlic, 82
    roast red pepper and smoked paprika, 81
    veg sticks and hummus, 182
hydration, 21

ingredient quality, 26

juices
    flu-fighter, 40
    ginger bug, 40
    green-eyed monster, 40

kale
    green-eyed monster juice, 40
    kale, roast butternut squash, quinoa and
       pomegranate salad, 126
kidney beans *see* beans
kitchen equipment, 24
knives, 24

lettuce
    charred baby gem, 112
    ginger bug juice, 40
    tender-stem broccoli, spinach, baby gem and
       vegetable crisps, 118
    Vietnamese rice paper rolls, 184

main courses
    baked cod with nettle pesto and cherry
       tomatoes, 140
    beef steak with salsa verde and rainbow
       chips, 156
    beetroot, feta and black bean burgers, 162
    bulgur wheat, quinoa and beetroot risotto, 160
    burrito beef bowl with Mexican bean salsa,
       146

butternut squash, walnut, feta and pesto tart,
    167
    chicken and beans, 136
    chicken and grain traybake, 142
    citrus chicken with broccoli rice, 152
    courgetti prawn, 138
    creamy apricot and almond turkey, 170
    creamy fish pie, 148
    crispy fish tacos, 172
    ginger, chicken and chickpea curry, 144
    goat's cheese, black olive, tomato and
    courgette tart, 166
    grilled salmon with pesto and roasted stuffed
       sweet potato, 154
    millet, butternut squash and linseed burgers,
       158–9
    red pepper, spinach and brie frittata, 168
    squash noodles with garlic prawns, 174
    sticky sesame pork and greens, 150
    Vietnamese filled coconut crepes, 164
meal planning, 13–14
Mediterranean quinoa and bulgur salad with
    shredded chicken, 116
Mediterranean style loaf, 56
mental health, 22
meringue kisses, 200–201
Mexican bean salsa, 146
millet, butternut squash and linseed burgers,
    158–9
mousses
    avocado and raspberry mousse cups, 192
    dark chocolate and orange mousse cups, 192
mozzarella *see* cheese
muffins
    berry and oat muffins, 68
mushrooms
    creamy garlic mushroom sauce, 157
    mushroom and fennel soup, 94

nettle and parmesan pesto, 84

oat and berry recharger, 42
oat and seed yoghurt loaf, 56

oats
    apple and cinnamon muesli, 32
    apple, pear and ginger crumble, 202

apricot and pecan flapjacks, 64
banana and oat pancakes, 48
berry and oat muffins, 68
bircher muesli, 32
carrot cake with yoghurt icing, 72
date caramel banoffee pie, 190–191
dark chocolate and walnut banana bread, 70
fluffy oat scones, 60
fruit and nut dark chocolate oaties, 66
granola, 30
Mediterranean style loaf, 56
oat and berry recharger, 42
oat and seed yoghurt loaf, 56
quinoa and oat banana bake, 36
olives
    goat's cheese, black olive, tomato and
        courgette tart, 166
    Mediterranean quinoa and bulgur salad with
        shredded chicken, 116

pancakes
    banana and oat pancakes, 48
    buckwheat pancakes, 46
parmesan *see* cheese
parmesan and garlic hummus, 80
parsnips
    rainbow chips, 156
    roast root vegetable and coriander soup, 92
pea, spinach and smoked bacon soup, 96
pears
    apple, pear and ginger crumble, 202
    roast honey fruits, 198
peas
    pea, spinach and smoked bacon soup, 96
pecans
    apricot and pecan flapjacks, 64
    cinnamon and pecan babhka rolls, 74–5
peppers
    red pepper, spinach and brie frittata, 168
    roast red pepper and smoked paprika
        hummus, 81
    roast tomato and red pepper soup, 102
pesto
    baked cod with nettle pesto and cherry
        tomatoes, 140
    basil and sunflower seed pesto, 84

butternut squash, walnut, feta and pesto tart,
    167
    coriander, cashew and walnut pesto, 83
    grilled salmon with pesto and roasted stuffed
        sweet potato, 154
    nettle and parmesan pesto, 84
physiotherapy, 10, 21
plums
    crunchy date and seed plum pots, 52
    roast honey fruits, 198
pomegranate
    kale, roast butternut squash, quinoa and
        pomegranate salad, 126
pork
    sticky sesame pork and greens, 150
    Vietnamese filled coconut crepes, 164
positivity, 22
potato salad with beetroot and almond, 112
prawns
    courgetti prawn, 138
    crispy Asian slaw with cod and roasted
        cashews, 128
    squash noodles with garlic prawns, 174
    Vietnamese filled coconut crepes, 164
    Vietnamese rice paper rolls, 184
prunes
    buckwheat and coconut prune bars, 178

quiches
    cupcake quiches, 34
quinoa *see* grains
quinoa and oat banana bake, 36

rainbow chips, 156
raspberries *see* berries
raspberry and almond coins, 62
red cabbage, carrot and seed slaw, 113
red pepper, spinach and brie frittata, 168
risottos
    bulgur wheat, quinoa and beetroot risotto, 160
roast carrot and garlic hummus, 82
roast honey fruits, 198
roast red pepper and smoked paprika hummus, 81
roast root vegetable and coriander soup, 92
roast tomato and red pepper soup, 102
roast vegetable and cranberry grains, 132
roasted stuffed sweet potato, 154

salads
  beetroot and mozzarella stacks, 123
  beetroot, freekeh, cucumber and mackerel,
    120
  broccoli and almond turmeric grains, 130
  broccoli, feta, tomato and hazelnut, 122
  carrot and seed slaw, 122
  cauliflower tabbouleh, 110
  charred baby gem, 112
  crispy Asian slaw with cod and roasted
    cashews, 128
  kale, roast butternut squash, quinoa and
    pomegranate, 126
  Mediterranean quinoa and bulgur salad with
    shredded chicken, 116
  potato salad with beetroot and almond, 112
  red cabbage, carrot and seed slaw, 113
  roast vegetable and cranberry grains, 132
  tender-stem broccoli, spinach, baby gem and
    vegetable crisps, 118
salsa verde, 156
sauces, dressings and dips
  basil and sunflower seed pesto, 84
  beetroot and mint hummus, 80
  cashew sauce, 159
  coriander, cashew and walnut pesto, 83
  creamy garlic mushroom sauce, 157
  creamy tahini dressing, 87
  dukkah, 85
  Frenchie dressing, 86
  guacamole, 87
  homemade nut butter, 88
  nettle and parmesan pesto, 84
  parmesan and garlic hummus, 80
  roast carrot and garlic hummus, 82
  roast red pepper and smoked paprika
  hummus, 81
  salsa verde, 156
  sweet chilli sauce, 86
scones
  berry scones, 58
  fluffy oat scones, 60
  seeded spelt scones, 58
seasonal food, 16
seeds
  apple, pear and ginger crumble, 202
  basil and sunflower seed pesto, 84

bircher muesli, 32
buckwheat and coconut prune bars, 178
carrot and seed slaw, 122
crunchy date and seed plum pots, 52
dukkah, 85
fruit and yoghurt with seed sprinkle, 182
granola, 30
millet, butternut squash and linseed burgers,
  158–9
oat and seed yoghurt loaf, 56
red cabbage, carrot and seed slaw, 113
seeded spelt scones, 58
self-belief, 7
side dishes
  Mexican bean salsa, 146
  rainbow chips, 156
  roasted stuffed sweet potato, 154
  spicy sweet potato wedges, 147
slaws see salads
smoked mackerel crush, 183
smoky baked beans with bacon and sourdough,
  44
smoothies
  banana and nut butter smoothie, 42
  oat and berry recharger, 42
snacks
  apple with nut butter, 182
  buckwheat and coconut prune bars, 178
  fruit and yoghurt with seed sprinkle, 182
  smoked mackerel crush, 183
  sweet potato toasts, 180
  veg sticks and hummus, 182
  Vietnamese rice paper rolls, 184
soups
  beetroot and carrot soup, 104
  creamy broccoli and cashew soup, 100
  creamy roast cauliflower soup, 106
  mushroom and fennel soup, 94
  pea, spinach and smoked bacon soup, 96
  roast root vegetable and coriander soup, 92
  roast tomato and red pepper soup, 102
  spiced butternut squash soup, 98
spelt
  seeded spelt scones, 58
  spelt babhka rolls, 74–5
spiced butternut squash soup, 98
spicy sweet potato wedges, 147

spinach
  pea, spinach and smoked bacon soup, 96
  red pepper, spinach and brie frittata, 168
  tender-stem broccoli, spinach, baby gem and
    vegetable crisps, 118
sport, 4–8
squash noodles with garlic prawns, 174
sterilisation, 24
stick blenders, 24
sticky sesame pork and greens, 150
storage containers, 24
strawberries see berries
strawberry and ginger yoghurt cups, 196
sugar, 12
sweet chilli sauce, 86
sweet potato toasts, 180
sweet potatoes
  creamy fish pie, 148
  grilled salmon with pesto and roasted stuffed
    sweet potato, 154
  roast root vegetable and coriander soup, 92
  spicy sweet potato wedges, 147
  sweet potato toasts, 180
sweetcorn see corn

tahini dressing, 87
tarts
  butternut squash, walnut, feta and pesto tart,
    167
  goat's cheese, black olive, tomato and
    courgette tart, 166
tender-stem broccoli, spinach, baby gem and
  vegetable crisps, 118
tomatoes
  bacon and balsamic roasted tomato flatbreads,
    38
  baked cod with nettle peso and cherry
    tomatoes, 140
  broccoli, feta, tomato and hazelnut salad, 122
  goat's cheese, black olive, tomato and
    courgette tart, 166

guacamole, 87
Mediterranean style loaf, 56
Mexican bean salsa, 146
roast tomato and red pepper soup, 102
turkey
  creamy apricot and almond turkey, 170
turnips
  ginger, chicken and chickpea curry, 144
  red pepper, spinach and brie frittata, 168
  roast root vegetable and coriander soup, 92

veg sticks and hummus, 182
Vietnamese filled coconut crepes, 164
Vietnamese rice paper rolls, 184

walnuts
  butternut squash, walnut, feta and pesto tart,
    167
  coriander, cashew and walnut pesto, 83
  dark chocolate and walnut banana bread, 70
white chocolate and raspberry bites, 76
white chocolate and raspberry cheesecake, 188

yoghurt
  bacon and balsamic roasted tomato flatbreads,
    38
  berry and oat muffins, 68
  butternut squash, walnut, feta and pesto tart,
    167
  carrot cake with yoghurt icing, 72
  coconut and berry sponge cake, 204
  crunchy date and seed plum pots, 52
  fruit and yoghurt with seed sprinkle, 182
  millet , butternut squash and linseed burgers,
    158
  oat and seed yoghurt loaf, 56
  roast honey fruits, 198
  smoked mackerel crush, 183
  strawberry and ginger yoghurt cups, 196